NIGEL TAYLOR   EDDY STIBBE   WILLIAM FOX-PITT   TINY CLAPHAM   KAREN DIXON

HELEN BELL   VIRGINIA ELLIOT   JANE HOUGHTON-BROWN   MARK BARRY   MARY KING

ANDREW NICHOLSON   ANDREAS WEISER   LUCINDA MURRAY   ANDREW BENNIE   RODNEY POWELL

ANDREW HOY   MIKE ETHERINGTON-SMITH   BLYTH TAIT   ANNA HERMANN   KAREN O'CONNOR

LESLIE LAW   ROBERT LEMIEUX   MARIE-CHRISTINE DUROY   DAISY DICK   CHARLOTTE BATHE

CAROLINE SIZER   VICTORIA LATTA   R STEWART CHRISTIE   MARK TODD   LYNNE BEVAN

VISIONS

— OF —

EVENTING

VISIONS

— OF —

EVENTING

ELIZABETH
FURTH

J. A. ALLEN Ltd

British Library Cataloguing-in-Publication Data.
A catalogue record for this book is available from the British Library.

ISBN 0 85131 662 X

Published in Great Britain in 1996 by
J. A. Allen & Company Limited,
1 Lower Grosvenor Place, Buckingham Palace Road,
London, SW1W OEL.

Designed by Design / Section, Frome
Printed by Dah Hua Printing Press Co. Ltd.,
Hong Kong

Dedication

For my family: without their love for horses, I would never have been inspired to pursue this career.

Acknowledgements

In particular, I would like to thank Chris Stafford for her support, encouragement and invaluable help!
I am also very grateful to Caroline Burt for believing in me and for her tactful, gentle but yet firm hand in ensuring that I met my deadline. My appreciation goes to all the riders for without their willing participation in sharing their anecdotes this book would never have been possible. Finally, the most valuable contributors have been the horses, the true stars of three day eventing.

Frontispiece: Lucinda Murray and Arctic Goose on the steeplechase at Badminton, 1994

CONTENTS

PREFACE

Compiling *Visions of Eventing* has given me the opportunity to learn more about the complexity of the sport. Although I had a little experience in Novice eventing myself, it is only since I have been photographing at international events that I have been able to develop a deeper understanding of what three day eventing is all about. It has given me the chance to develop greater compassion for the sport as well as for the riders' way of life. Hard work, determination, dedication and the acquired knowledge are qualities which are common to riders, course designers and judges alike, all drawn out by the deep passion they feel for horses and eventing. I have found out that the hours spent in the saddle, getting to know the horses and teaching them the different disciplines, together with the love of competing, is what gives the event riders most pleasure. A lot of them strive for perfection and will seek professional advice in the different disciplines as much as they can in order to achieve their goals.

Talking to dressage judge Jane Houghton-Brown has been an eye opener because it has revealed the complexity and the degree of responsibility a judge holds during the entire duration of a three day event. Meeting cross country course designer Mike Etherington-Smith has not only reinforced the importance of his work with regards to training and the safety of horse and rider but it also shows the accountability of his position. While interviewing show jumping course designer Alan Oliver I was reminded of philosophies expressed by the course designers I had spoken to for my first book *Visions of Show Jumping*. None the less, although parallels can be drawn, different aspects and considerations have to be accounted for when building the show jumping course for a three day event.

Most of the riders featured in this book saw their pictures for the first time when I met them and it was wonderful to feel their spontaneous support and encouragement. It was also fascinating to witness to what extent a photograph triggered off memories and emotions alike. This also goes for those riders I had to interview over the phone because they didn't come to England while I was writing the book.

Producing *Visions of Eventing* has given me a lot of pleasure and I hope that you will enjoy the photographs as well as the numerous contributions that the riders have made. Not only have they revealed their horse's character by sharing interesting anecdotes but, by doing so, they have also generously given insight into their own personalities.

FOREWORD

It is with great pleasure and a great honour to be invited to write the foreword to Elizabeth Furth's second book, *Visions of Eventing*, a companion volume to her first book, *Visions of Show Jumping*.

Written with great knowledge and understanding of the three day event, this book reveals the innermost feelings of several extremely talented and modest leading competitors, some of whom readily admit to knowing their horses better than their spouses!

In addition to these fascinating insights are the objective views of some of the most knowledgeable experts in the disciplines that go to make up the three day event.

Elizabeth Furth deserves all congratulations for producing this most passionate and readable book.

The day after Karen O'Connor and Mr Maxwell did their dressage test at the 1992 Badminton Horse Trials, the US rider had to endure 'the worst day of my life'. During the cross country, the pair missed their line at the Vicarage Vee, which resulted in a fatal fall for the Irish gelding.

'Mr Maxwell had been very tense the whole week and particularly uptight during his dressage test. It was a windy day and the whole atmosphere of Badminton had just been a little bit too overwhelming for him. Having to destroy him the next day after the fall was horrible. He was a very sensitive horse who didn't relate well to people but communicated very well with both me and his groom. He had a wonderful personality, a huge heart and he would always try to give his very best. In training, you could never criticise him for not trying enough because if you did you would shatter his confidence. You always had to reward him rather then telling him that what he did wasn't good enough. He was such a great friend'

9

THE
DRESSAGE

The dressage is the first discipline of a three day event. Because of the number of competitors at major international events, the dressage is usually held over the first two days, the Thursday and Friday of the competition. Horses and riders perform an FEI (Fédération Equestre Internationale) three day event dressage test, comprising twenty individually marked movements. Three judges award a maximum of ten marks to each of those movements as well as to four collective scores. Freedom and regularity of paces, impulsion, submission and position and seat of the rider and the correct use of the aids fall into this category and are scrutinised during the test. The highest score any event rider could ever obtain from the dressage test is 240 marks. As the second and third competition days are scored in penalty points, however, the average total of dressage marks are subtracted from the maximum possible and multiplied by 0.6 to give the penalty score.

The dressage phase is an essential element within the sport and to the competitors it has become increasingly important in relation to the remaining two disciplines. Dressage has always held an important place in the training of horses, its objective being to improve the athletic ability as well as the outline of the horse. The better the horse is schooled, the calmer and more supple it will become

and it will therefore have a greater chance of achieving absolute understanding with its rider. Within the context of the three day event the dressage test should demonstrate the horse's obedience, suppleness and freedom of forward movement.

At this level of competition, however, riders are performing on extremely fit horses, some of which are highly strung which demands a sensitive approach to achieve the required balance between creating and controlling impulsion to achieve the necessary collection. After all, the word 'dressage' is French and means taming or training. Therefore, a sound training does not only give the riders the desired control over their horses but it also sets the foundation for the challenges that are presented in the phases which follow. A good test will be rewarded with top marks and give the riders an excellent starting point for the remaining disciplines. Although some of the best cross country horses can show certain weaknesses in the dressage, riders always aim to maximise on the horse's potential in order to have a chance of finishing high up in the classification. One often hears of the satisfaction riders get from finishing a three day event on their dressage score, meaning that no extra penalty points were collected during the other phases. If the horse's

Badminton 1994

dressage is as well developed as its cross country and show jumping skills, the chance of a top spot in the final line up seems almost certain. Although some horses can make up the deficit of a poor dressage test by having a faultless speed and endurance, the standard of dressage has significantly improved over recent years and riders agree that they can no longer rely solely on good jumping.

Riders usually spend hours preparing their horses for the dressage test, the difficulty being that the fitter the horse is, the longer it generally needs to settle down before it is relaxed enough to accept the rider's aids. Getting a top competition horse into the right frame of mind for the job is part of the

Leslie Law and Welton Apollo, Badminton, 1991 – Leslie struggles to get into his dressage tails while Welton Apollo enjoys a final polish before their dressage test

rider's art. Preparing a horse for the occasion is very much a case of knowing the horse's character, its likes, dislikes, strengths and weaknesses. More and more competitors rely on the help of a personal dressage trainer who advises them at home as well as on the day. The working-in period before the test is crucial. A horse can be too fresh, overworked or bored and therefore off the boil or, ideally, just right, attentive and obedient as well as willing to show off its paces. Some horses get terribly wound up when they sense the atmosphere of a competition and for their riders it's like sitting on a time bomb that can explode at any time and for no apparent reason. With other horses, big occasions can bring out the best in them and enhance their potential, resulting in a superb performance.

While talking to the riders it was interesting to find out that they all have their different views on dressage. The majority recognise its value as a means of schooling horses as well as its place in the context of the competition. Some would welcome changes to the method of judging and question the objectivity or, rather, subjectivity of it. Most riders gave the impression that they find the test boring and wanted some of the movements, such as the counter canter, taken out. Many felt that the flying change should be reintroduced because riders would have to teach their horses the movement and could then perhaps avoid the embarrassment of riding round the show jumping course in counter canter.

Spectators are usually scarce on the dressage days, not only because the tests are performed before the weekend and many people cannot afford to take time off work, but also because it's not the most spectacular discipline to watch. Compared to pure dressage, the three day event tests certainly lack flair and panache. The absence of more collected movements, such as piaffe, passage or canter pirouette add to the rather limited interest of the general public. Even from a photographic point of view, it is true that the higher movements lend themselves to more expressive pictures. Following a pirouette through my lens inspires me to a greater extent and presents a bigger challenge than photographing the less difficult movements of an event test. Apart from the odd occasion when horses blow up during a test, the trot and canter extensions are usually the most colourful moments to capture. However, knowing that the disciplines to come will produce more action, revealing the ultimate test of the sport, I am mostly on the look out for atmospheric shots in and around the warming-up area and only photograph the main contenders riding their test. I always feel that it is important not to disturb the rider or

horse's concentration while they are preparing for their test and therefore prefer to use a telephoto lens (300 mm) to capture candid shots.

Although the three judges on duty essentially agree on the principles of dressage, judging is inevitably a subjective art. Judges are positioned at three different locations and will therefore watch from slightly different angles, giving them another opinion or perspective which adds to their individual interpretation and marking.

In the following interview, dressage judge Jane Houghton-Brown shares her views on dressage while giving more detailed explanations of what is required of an event horse.

Robert Lemieux gets a helping hand from his daughter Kaylee to prepare for the dressage at Badminton in 1988

Jane Houghton-Brown

Jane Houghton-Brown is a highly respected FEI
(Fédération Equestre Internationale) horse trials
judge and has been appointed president of the ground
jury at numerous top three day events. Her time is
now divided among judging, training and chairing the
British Horse Society (BHS) Training and Education
Committee. She is also a Fellow of the BHS.

Although Jane was born into a non-horsy family,
she always knew that she wanted a career with horses
when she left school. 'My interest in horses came
from within. I used to pester my parents to take me
to pubs where there were horses so that I could get
on them.' Soon after, she enjoyed a successful show

jumping career during which she was runner up to
Harvey Smith as the Show Jumper of the Year in 1965.
Winter months were spent point-to-pointing and she
also had a couple of Advanced event horses on which
she was 'quite successful' in three day events. As if
this did not keep her busy enough, she started taking
'a few BHS exams because it was the thing to do'. She
admits that although she has done a bit of combined
training, her main interest was jumping and she
wasn't particularly clued up about the dressage. In her
early twenties she had the opportunity to take the
horse on which she was planning to compete at
Badminton for some dressage lessons with Hungarian
trainer Tibor Demko Belanski.

As far as the care of horses is concerned, Jane is
really 'self- taught' and considers herself a late
starter. She remembers nurturing her concern for the
horse's welfare by reading up on the subject, in
particular the veterinary side as it had always been of
special interest. Jane carried on jumping until she
was pregnant with her first son and, being at a loose
end during her pregnancy, she decided to start
teaching by getting involved with the Essex and
Suffolk Pony Club, training their eventing teams. It
was then that her transition to dressage really came
about because she realised that, 'If you wanted to
teach people, they were not going to pay you to teach
jumping. What they wanted was to learn dressage.'
Encouraged by this, Jane sought help with her own
dressage and was influenced by Dietmar Ackermann,
Franz Rochawansky and Ferdi Eilberg. At the same
time Jane was placed on the BHS judges lists and

soon progressed to List One, which entitles her to judge Grand Prix.

Being ambitious, Jane enquired about how to get on to the International Judges List for three day eventing and found out that one has to compile a CV. The International Equestrian Federation (FEI) requires that a person be a minimum List Four dressage judge, with some experience in eventing as a rider, trainer or judge. Jane qualified on more than one count and became an FEI Horse Trials Judge in 1990 which enables her to judge all over the world. There is, however, a further step up to the top FEI list which allows judges to officiate at Olympic Games and major championships. Although she would love to judge a major championship, Jane is also very realistic about it and feels that she has actually done far more than she could have reasonably expected. Apart from having judged at major events in Britain, such as Windsor, Blenheim, Burghley and Gatcombe, she has also judged in Belgium, Holland, Canada and the United States.

Being a judge at a three day event goes beyond assessing the competitor's dressage test. The three appointed judges also represent the ground jury whose responsibilities include far more than the average eventing fan might expect. 'The members of the ground jury assemble two days before the competition begins and inspect phases A, B, C and D of the speed and endurance. We have to ensure that the flags are correctly placed, the obstacles meet the criteria for the competition we are about to judge and, above all, that the fences are safe. It is only a

check because the appointed technical delegate walks round with us and he will already have verified the course. In Britain it is most unlikely that one would meet a major problem but in other countries that are not as experienced we need to be a little more vigilant and sometimes may have to make big adjustments like changing the dimensions of fences or taking one out all together. We have to check that phases A and C (the roads and tracks) are correctly signposted so that the riders will find their way round. We inspect the location of the ten-minute box and that it has all the facilities required. We also check the stopping points on the steeplechase, ensure there is adequate water and where the farrier is going to be located.

'We inspect the dressage arena, that it's correctly marked and that the judges' huts are in the right position. It is necessary to be flexible, especially when you go to countries where they don't have organised and well-trained volunteers on hand. Although everything should be ready for our initial inspection, it's not always possible so we have to negotiate when we arrive and we may have to get involved ourselves. We have all erected flags, tidied up brush fences and done all sorts of other things in the lead up to an event at some stage!

'Then the stables have to be inspected to make sure they are suitable. We have to fill in a report in which everything has to be mentioned, even the competitors' showers. The veterinary inspection is the next duty, when we have to ensure that the horses are sound enough to compete. Although a vet is always present in an advisory capacity, it's the ground jury's responsibility and they have the final say. For me, one of the fascinations is that you see these horses for one minute when they are trotting up and, within that minute, you have to make a quick appraisal: "Is it fit? Is it sound?" and, just for fun you ask yourself, "Is it a nice horse?"

'The following day we move on to the dressage phase itself and the good thing is that because we have seen the horses trot up, we have a list and I always make little comments. For example, it could be that a horse may have been slightly unlevel, or there might be something about the horse that impresses me. So if anything strikes me during their dressage test, I have a reference. We may find out that the horse had to trot twice at the inspection but that we decided to pass it. So if you are concerned about its dressage, you can refer the horse to the vet and have it checked before it starts phase A.

'On the speed and endurance day, it's our responsibility to ensure that everything happens on time. During the cross country section itself you go to phases A and B to watch two or three horses go before going back to the ten-minute box. Then the three members of the ground jury will separate. The president may stay in or near to the control box while another member will be with the vet at the end of phase C to watch the horses coming into the box. You get a feel for the way things are running, how the weather affects the horses and keep an eye on them while they are in the ten minute box. It is the ground jury's responsibility to stop a horse if, in conjunction

with the vet, you decide it should not continue. It is then our responsibility to tell the rider that they will not be allowed to carry on. Usually the person in the box will also observe the way that the horses are finishing phase D. The third member is out on the course to monitor the competitors.

'On the Sunday morning we assemble to check the horses for the final inspection. The ground jury, in conjunction with the vet, also agrees on which horses should be dope tested. It's done at random in as much as we don't necessarily test the first three. We would refer to our notes and one does get pretty cute at spotting whether you think that a horse has been given something. I have only ever had one horse dope tested positive. We usually test one or two after the end of the first two days but leave them after the end of the cross country day because they are tired, and test another one or two after the show jumping. We also make sure that the show jumping course is suitable for the level of the competition and then, of course, we judge that final phase.'

Jane can very easily point out the difference in judging pure dressage and dressage for eventing. 'Looking at a dressage test for a four-star three day event, where you have shoulder-in, half pass and going up and down the gears, the main difference is that we are asking event horses to work through the lateral movements without collection. This said, it is, of course, impossible to come down the centre line and halt from canter, ride an extension or do half pass without a certain degree of collection. Because event dressage has changed a great deal over the past few years, the differences are getting smaller and we are looking for the same degree of engagement in the four-star test as we are looking for from a Medium dressage horse. If the event horse hasn't got that degree of engagement, it's not going to have the self-carriage, nor the ability to really utilise its paces to its fullest potential. We cannot tolerate horses that are not regular or are uneven in the step sequence of any of their three paces. We have a little more latitude on the obedience in as much as if a horse makes a slightly excited transition, or if it has a little shy, it's not quite as serious providing the quality of the work is good because we appreciate that these horses are extremely fit. A few years ago, as long as the event horse was obedient, had correct basic training, it didn't even matter whether it was a good mover. But today it does! Riders have become a great deal better trained, they know more about how to train horses so therefore the standard has actually improved. Consequently the judges' expectations have increased. Our own horses in Britain have changed tremendously. Whereas the Germans could always beat us, they can't anymore. Nowadays the event horse is more engaged, more up in front and, as a result, its self-carriage has also improved.'

Jane has specific criteria by which she judges the dressage at a three day event. 'The first thing I will be impressed with is a horse that has been correctly trained, is in front of the leg, into the rein and in self-carriage. If he has got that as a base, even if he is not a quality mover, I'm still going to feel very friendly towards him, and I'll be wanting to award him sevens. If, on top of that, he is a quality mover, I'll be able to offer more eights and nines. The dressage judge has to be very aware of how they award the marks. The FEI encourages us to have a difference of sixty marks between the top and bottom horses because by the time the multiplying factor and the coefficient are applied, the gap gets narrowed down anyway. One shouldn't bunch the mediocre horses all together in one group but try and

Brynley Powell considering his marks after the dressage test at Burghley in 1994

Mary King and friends delighted with King Kong after their dressage test at Burghley in 1994

separate them. A horse might be better because it's accepting the bit although it can't actually show a medium trot. We have to give horses credit for what they can do.

'Purely from an eventing point of view, I'm looking for a horse that is sixteen to sixteen-one hands at the most, an athlete that can adjust his balance very easily but, again, there is no substitute for correct and good training, no matter what the discipline. For me this is why the New Zealand riders have the edge because they are horsemen through and through. They can ride the dressage as well as the cross country and the show jumping.'

Jane puts a lot of emphasis on the importance of dressage within the sport of three day eventing and would not like to see it go. 'One of the great strengths of dressage is the way in which, through systematic training, it builds up the horse's physique in the correct way. Because the horse's frame is then correctly developed, its competitive life can be more assured. Clearly, the better balanced a horse is, the less stress there is on joints and muscles and therefore the horse will last much longer. Mark Todd's Charisma, for example, was beautifully trained and lasted for years. So, if we took out the dressage, we would lose out, even from a show jumping point of view. We just have to look at the show jumpers; they can all produce a decent medium test and do the flying change as four and five year olds. It's ridiculous that event horses can't do the flying change and I would like to see it reintroduced at four star level.

'Taking the dressage away would be disastrous and substituting it with anything else wouldn't work for me either! Dressage is not only a test of obedience, it is vital for the athletic development of the horse. It helps the horse to perform better because it improves its muscle structure. Just like dancers don't just dance the ballet, they actually do all the floor exercises first to ensure that their bodies are in the right shape to perform. Horses are the same; they must have the foundation from which they can progress into various areas.

'If you want to win, you've got to be good at all three phases. Riders cannot rely on jumping a double clear within the time; that will leave them in the placings but not get them in the winner's slot. They have to ensure they get the dressage as good as they possibly can. No matter what the level of eventing, the dressage and show jumping should be polished so that horses and riders only have to concentrate on the cross country which is always a bit of an unknown factor.'

Jane enjoys judging events immensely and has made the training and studying of eventing her life. However, she is still fascinated with judging pure dressage and considers it a good thing to help to keep her eye in. With regards to the role of the dressage judges in eventing, Jane would like to give training courses. 'In this country we have a lot of judges who are not especially geared up towards it. They go to normal judging courses on training for dressage tests, but they don't look at the eventing tests which are made up differently.'

Mary King (née Thomson) and King William represented Great Britain at the 1992 Barcelona Olympic Games. Thanks to their elegant test, the pair took fourth place after the dressage and helped the British team into the lead before the cross country day.

'King William was extremely fit and just bursting to go in Barcelona which meant that I had to ride him for a long time before the dressage. Not so much to exhaust him but just to try and get him to relax. Although we were scheduled for six o'clock in the evening, I rode him on and off throughout the day, trying to calm him down. During the entire test he was on the verge of exploding, which is when he is at his most impressive, but he was just a little overpowering and too strong. Still, he is such a cool dude. His elegance gets him many fans. He reminds me of a city gent with dark hair, wearing a dark suit and tie. A lot of girls are after him but so am I and I'm fighting them all off!'

After a 'diabolical dressage test' at the
1992 Barcelona Olympics, Blyth Tait
fought back like a lion to secure the
individual bronze medal. His efforts on
Messiah were also welcomed by the
bronze-medal-winning Kiwi team.

'The disaster occurred earlier in the
week when Messiah had bruised his sole.
We had put special pads under his shoe
but on the way to the arena the shoe had
moved and caused pressure on the area.
We had to remove the shoe several times
before he didn't feel discomfort any
more. This meant that there was no time
to work him in prior to our test. He went
into the arena completely unprepared and
took full advantage of the situation.
Sitting on top, I just wished that I wasn't
there! The only reason why I felt that I
should ride was that the team was so
supportive which certainly eased the
blow. Furthermore, it just goes to show
that one should never give up. Messiah
was usually volatile in the dressage but
he also had the ability to lead after his
test as he had done at several horse
trials. But if he was in the mood, he
could also take the mickey to the extent
that we could finish up near the bottom'

Ian Stark and Glenburnie were in thirty-fourth position after the dressage and although they had gone clear across country, Ian decided to withdraw the horse before the final test. Winning a team and an individual gold medal at the 1991 European Championships as well as a second place at Badminton in 1988 qualify as their best achievements.

'The one time Glenburnie did a good dressage test was when he won the European Championship in Punchestown and that was because we went early in the morning and there was not a soul around the arena. It was quiet and he thought that he was still working in. If his temperament would have let him relax in an arena, he would have been unbeatable. I had him on homoeopathic pills to try and keep him relaxed but still, whenever he got into the crowds, he would just blow up. When this happens while you're doing your test, you just feel that you are in the arena for a month! Glenburnie was the fastest event horse I have ever ridden and had the most incredible stamina. He was bred to be a Gold Cup horse and I "stole" him from the owners. I'm quite sure that he would have been a Desert Orchid but he didn't do a bad job going eventing!'

Metronome is owned by trainer Ruth McMullen for whom
Pippa Funnell worked for several years. Being 'the mad one
who got to sit on the youngsters that really bucked',
Pippa was asked to break in Metronome as a three year
old. Although Pippa moved away when she married show
jumper William Funnell, she has kept the ride on
Metronome. Their biggest triumph to date is winning the
1993 Blenheim Audi International Horse Trials.

'I remember being bucked off Metronome one day and
landing on my knees about three inches away from a stone
wall! But he has developed into a horse that is very happy
in his work. He is a lovely horse to ride and when he's
going how you want him, he's a dream to sit on. He's a

very flashy mover and so light off the floor. He is a
complete gentleman to handle. You can even clip him
when he's lying down. Metronome has got the most
wonderful character and if he could, he'd live in the house
with us.'

Mark Todd and Just An Ace endured the dressage test at the 1994 Badminton Horse Trials. A score of 57.2 put them into twenty-second place, some 19.8 points behind German rider Marina Loheit who led the field. However, all was not lost and the pair made up for it in the remaining phases, finishing the competition in fifth place.

'I don't particularly enjoy dressage on Just An Ace because it feels to me like I could lose everything at any time. He is actually quite difficult in the dressage and can get a little tense. He doesn't find the dressage work easy as he can be quite stiff and rigid, but he still manages to produce a fairly good test. He will never win the dressage but he will always be thereabouts, providing you get him on a good day!'

Ian Stark remembered that Murphy Himself 'had done a most brilliant dressage test' at Badminton in 1991 and couldn't relate to this particular split second. Ian does, however, admit that whenever Murphy thought that he was being restrained, he would just take off into the air.

'If you got his working-in right, he was very obedient in the dressage but if he was at all fresh, then you could look out. He was very keen on fly bucking! You couldn't actually ride him anywhere to and from gallops and feel safe. I was loaned a heart monitor and I put it on Murphy one day. We were heading towards the gallops, only walking and trotting along the road for half an hour. As we came down to where we start the gallop, the alarm went off! This was very typical for Murphy, he did get pretty wound up about life!'

THE STEEPLECHASE

The second test of a three day event is dedicated to the endurance phase for horses and riders. After having loosened up their horses on the first roads and tracks, competitors arrive at the steeplechase, the first real assessment of speed, stamina and jumping ability. A distance, usually, of about 3,000 metres has to be ridden at the set speed of 690 metres per minute which means that horses are galloping and jumping brush fences at full stretch for between four and four and a half minutes. Although there has been some controversy about the distance of the steeplechase and some riders would like it to be shortened, especially in hot and humid conditions, most riders do agree that the steeplechase makes a valuable contribution and has a definite role within the framework of the competition. The steeplechase has been designed to test the horse's stamina and ability to tackle fences at racing speed but, more to the point and in relation to the rest of the test, its other aim is to set up horses and riders for the cross country phase. A lot of competitors will tell you that they get a real kick out of riding at speed and that the necessary aggression puts them in the right frame of mind. Others will admit that on some horses it can be a hair-raising experience for fear of not finding the brakes! However, one thing is certain, a good steeplechase round puts horses and riders on a high

To improve on her steeplechase technique, US rider Karen O'Connor rides out racehorses whenever she can. Together with the English-bred gelding Prince Panache, who is a half-brother to Mary King's King William, they came fifth at Burghley in 1994. 'Prince Panache is a beautiful jumper. He is very similar to a racehorse and can get very strong in the steeplechase. The last thing you want to do then is start having a struggle because that will only make him work too hard. My strongest aid at that point would be to reach down to give him a reassuring pat and tell him that it's all right or to soften my hands to him. Then you can feel him taking a deep breath and settling back down again. He has enormous courage, he's very cat-like and careful in his jumping and yet he is tremendously powerful with it. But he also has very low self-esteem and he doesn't believe in himself as much as I believe in him. The first two years I had him the emphasis was on telling him that he's good at his job. Now he is looking at life a lot more positively. With this newly acquired attitude, the sky is the limit for Prince Panache'

Kathryn Harris and The Coaley Fox on the roads and tracks at Windsor in 1995

and also gives them confidence. A bad round, on the other hand, can not only put them out of the competition all together, but can also cause doubt which disturbs the rider's as well as the horse's confidence.

Riding a steeplechase requires yet another skill in the complex discipline of three day eventing – the ability to know how to gallop a horse without tiring it or using up your own strength. To perfect the art of

saving energy, combined with adapting to the required speed, many of the top riders will have ridden out racehorses at some stage of their career. US rider Karen O'Connor feels that the steeplechase is something in which she continually improves with every three day event she competes in. Top riders put a lot of emphasis on learning the correct racing position. It is, in fact, a true art to stay in a good rhythm at the right speed and still be within about three seconds of the optimum time, which is what every rider ultimately tries to achieve. Having an erratic round on the steeplechase can disrupt the rhythm of horse and rider. The main objective from a horseman's point of view is to keep one pace and have the horses running and jumping effortlessly so that it takes as little out of them as possible. In the overall context of the speed and endurance day, a smooth steeplechase round makes a big difference to the final stages of the cross country course because riders will have saved their horse's energy without incurring time penalties.

From a photographer's point of view, I have always found it most frustrating that, due to the timetable of the different phases, I can spend only a limited amount of time on the steeplechase for fear of missing the start of the cross country. However, I always make a point of catching the first seven to ten riders on phase B and, if I am lucky, those competitors will be top riders who have entered two horses. Otherwise, the main contenders are usually scheduled towards the end of the field when it is impossible to rush back and forth. I get a lot of satisfaction out of capturing competitors at speed. Not only do you get a fairly accurate idea of how fast horses are actually travelling, but it is also a fabulous experience seeing them at such close range. Following the horses at full stretch through a telephoto lens where horse and rider fill the entire frame is wonderfully exciting. You can really feel the force and power that horses possess. When I'm out on the steeplechase, my prime challenge is trying to freeze the moment in which the horse shows its athletic potential and the rider their concentration. Watching and photographing riders like Mark Todd at work on the steeplechase is a privilege. Mark really gives the impression of just letting his horse run underneath him; he perfects the art of simultaneously containing and releasing the horse's energy without disturbing its rhythm. Furthermore, he must have a built-in clock because I have hardly ever seen him check his stopwatch! As for taking photographs over steeplechase fences, horses don't jump them in great style because, ideally, they should brush through them in order not to waste too much time in the air. Horses are galloping lower in comparison to the way they run during the cross country and therefore make a flatter shape over their fences. Riders have to prove their courage early on the steeplechase because trying to break the horse's rhythm, slowing it down or checking its stride in front of a steeplechase fence can result in disaster!

I do find it a shame that the steeplechase course is not better attended by the public because it gives the spectator a broader picture of the different demands of the speed and endurance phase. Most people only see the competitors on the cross country course but having watched them on the steeplechase makes you appreciate their athleticism even more. From a spectator's point of view, I can assure you that it's quite spectacular. To use Dorothy Trapp's (world silver medallist of 1994) words: 'It's one of the few times that you are allowed to just rock and roll and let it rip!'

Mark Todd and Michaelmas Day stayed clear inside the time
on the steeplechase at Badminton in 1990 but went on to
fall at fence eight of the cross country before retiring two
fences later. The cross country course had been shortened
by 800 metres that year to allow horses to recover quicker
in view of the Stockholm World Equestrian Games which
were held two months later. 'Michaelmas Day was terrifying
to ride on the steeplechase! He was just terrifying to ride
full stop! He was so strong, he'd pull like fury and was
sometimes less than careful at his obstacles. He did get
better as he got older. He should have just about won
Badminton one year but tipped up and fell at the Vicarage

Pond on the cross country. But I won an awful lot on him.
We used to have the odd tip up because he was so
exhuberant but would forget a leg. Frederick Bergendorff
rode him at the European Championship in 1993 and they
were members of the Swedish gold medal team. Sadly, he
died in 1994 of a twisted gut'

Having taken over the ride of Just An Ace from Robert Lemieux, Gloucestershire-based New Zealand rider Mark Todd took him to his first Badminton in 1991. The pair stayed clear and within the time on the steeplechase but exceeded the optimum time by a fraction on their otherwise faultless cross country round. Completing the competition in fifth place proved the beginning of their successful partnership.

'Just an Ace is a wonderful jumper, but not the fastest thing on four legs. He really only has one cruising speed. Steeplechase speed is very near his cruising speed and he is pretty much at full stretch all the way to get inside the time. I don't think it's his favourite phase but he is such a good jumper that it doesn't present a problem'

After having won Badminton in 1993, Ginny Elliot took Welton Houdini to the European Championship in Achselschwang, Germany. Although this picture was taken during the steeple-chase at Windsor in 1990, where the pair finished ninth, seeing Houdini on that phase prompted Ginny to remember the disaster that cost them the European title.

'Houdini had come to Achselschwang fitter than he had ever been. He already felt on edge, leaping around while we were warming up for the dressage, which was unlike him. As we came round the bend to fence two on the steeplechase, a very excited crowd rose from their seats and began cheering and clapping. Houdini was just totally fazed by the spectators. He locked his jaw and went straight past the fence. I had both reins in one hand trying to steer him round but there was absolutely nothing I could do! I had to circle and kick him over it. We collected twenty penalties plus some time faults and I could have absolutely shot him! He then proceeded to jump a brilliant round across country and we had the second fastest time without even trying. He did finish up seventh but it cost us the title. Somehow steeplechase and Houdini just don't go hand in hand!'

Spinning Rhombus and New Zealand rider Andrew Nicholson
have been a pair for more than seven years which, according to
Andrew, is quite rare as he tends to sell horses as soon as he
has taken them to the top. Although Spinning Rhombus let his
rider down terribly in the final phase of the Barcelona
Olympics, by collecting 45 jumping faults, he still holds a
special place in Andrew's heart. At the 1994 Burghley Rémy
Martin Horse Trials, they were first on the course and stayed
clear all the way, finishing in seventh place and on their
dressage score. ·

    'I doubt whether there is a horse around as good across
country as Spinning Rhombus. He runs on sheer courage. He
doesn't have much athletic ability but makes up for it with an
absolutely amazing amount of courage. He couldn't jump me out
of trouble through talent alone like some horses do, he would
just do it with his heart. He is the most confident horse I have
ever walked into the ten-minute box with. On the steeplechase I

always like to start at a slower speed than what I would finish
with. I just like to gradually build my speed up and maybe be a
few seconds late on the first minute. On Spinning Rhombus I
don't panic if I am ten seconds late when I reach the first
minute; I can just sit there knowing that he will pick up on
speed. At Burghley, however, I was getting slightly worried after
three minutes but I didn't want to chase him because I know
that he gets the speed up gradually by himself and still makes it
with a few minutes to spare. Spinning Rhombus is just so
experienced now. It also feels as if he has seen every sort of
jump which has made him into a hardened professor, cool and
calm. He judges a fence as soon as he sees it, and knows that if
a fence isn't too high it's because it must have a very big drop'

Caroline Sizer doesn't have the fondest memories of her 1990 visit to Badminton. Her mount Ghost Town lost a shoe at the water on the cross country day and although the horse seemed well enough to be presented for the final vet check, 'he must have had a slightly bruised sole' which resulted in the ground jury spinning him at the trot up.

'Ghost Town is usually really nice to ride on the steeplechase because he is always in front of the bridle. He can get a bit strong especially round the tight turns at the top end. I'm sure that Ghost Town thinks he is a biker because of the way he just throws himself round those bends! I sometimes lose him round the turn and then we are off like a rocket! None the less, I like the steeplechase because it warms the horses up and gets them going. It also helps me to get my eye in and when you're going round Badminton you need to know that your horse is jumping well. The steeplechase just confirms that everything is OK'

(Right) After having ridden Murphy Himself slowly to get him 'sort of in control' at one day events in preparation for Badminton in 1991, Ian Stark set off on the steeplechase in an American gag only to find out that the whole experience was 'a pretty fast one'. 'Murphy Himself bolted and I had neither steering nor brakes during the entire steeplechase, which was the most terrifying experience I have ever had! He wasn't always like that. He was, however, very fast and didn't have a lot of respect for his steeplechase fences. He would be quite happy to plough through them by the roots because he knew that they would give way before him. Steeplechase was a necessary evil for Murphy and to be honest, I'd rather go cross country than steeplechase on him!'

(Left) Ian Stark at Badminton in 1990

THE CROSS COUNTRY

Without a doubt, the cross country is the most exciting part of the three day event. After having been on the second roads and tracks, which is meant to be a recovery phase after the steeplechase, competitors finally reach the start of phase D. Once they have been thoroughly checked by a vet and the ground jury in the ten-minute box, riders get the go ahead to start on the cross country course. During those ten minutes, horses are cared for by the rider's team of helpers. They are stripped off and sponged down before the tack, including the all-important boots and bandages, is put back on. The legs are covered in Vaseline to protect the horses from getting grazed if they scrape the timber fences. It also helps them to slide over the fences more easily if they get stuck. While all of this is happening, riders will try to find out as much as they can about how the course is riding, if any fences have been causing trouble and whether the optimum time has been achieved. Riders who are also team members will discuss their instructions with the team manager and seek advice from other helpers who have been watching the competition.

The tension and anticipation which riders feel are at their most intense at the start of phase D. They will try to run the entire course through their minds, remembering the routes they are going to take at each fence. Stopwatches are set, the riders' adrenalin and nerves begin to take hold, but once the starter calls them into the start box and counts them down from ten seconds, much of the tension disappears. Concentration takes over as the mutual trust and confidence between horse and rider begin to appear. The relief of completing the cross country course is enormous because bringing your mount home safely is what the sport is all about. Achieving a clear round within the optimum time is a goal only few accomplish but when they do the elation those riders feel is unique. The cross country certainly offers riders the ultimate challenge and gives spectators the thrill of watching superfit horses galloping across country over solid fences.

From a photographic point of view the cross country offers a variety of opportunities. It becomes a real challenge to try to be at the right fence at the right time because the photos that sell most are the ones of leading riders jumping well over impressive fences or, in some cases, when the main contenders have had the misfortune of hitting the deck. My job can get quite stressful and I am usually tense on the morning of the cross country. After having walked the course on one of the previous days, I will attempt to look at some of the fences again to make sure that I have chosen a good fence from where to start. At

Before Ginny took over Griffin, the horse had fallen at the water in Saumur with his previous rider Ian Stark. When he stopped with Ginny while schooling him at Weston Park, she had her doubts about swapping Murphy for him.

'This photograph, taken at Badminton 1991, shows what a good jumping technique Griffin had over a fence. He basculed beautifully, really using his back and his neck, but that was his downfall because although he could jump quite high, he lacked a lot of scope widthways. Unless you met fences correctly, he would stop. He certainly didn't have the intention of jumping something that he thought was a little bit too big for him. He really disappointed me at the World Equestrian Games at Stockholm in 1990. He had gone clear and was on time up to five fences from home when he decided to put down between a parallel of hedges, a perfectly ordinary spread. Although he was placed in the first ten at Badminton, it would be fair to say that he didn't have enough guts to compete at four-star-level events'

**Georgie Caldwell and Welton
Abbey, Badminton, 1991**

the same time, I will go through the start list to
check the times when riders are most likely to be at
the fences I have chosen to photograph. I find it
impossible to walk round the entire course and get
good pictures at every fence. Some fences are not as
photogenic as others – they could be obscured by

trees – and some let-up fences are not very
spectacular. So a lot of thought goes into deciding
who to catch at which fence in order to ensure a good
selection of quality shots. Choosing when to walk
from one fence to another also comes into account
because missing one of the top riders, due to bad

planning, can be rather frustrating. It is, of course, tempting, especially in bad weather conditions, to stay all day at a fence which is certain to provide the most dramatic pictures. Usually this would be the water complex and I do, of course, cover it at some stage during the competition, but I make a point of resisting staying there all the time in order to get a selection of photographs at different fences. Besides, it would be too boring and I enjoy seeing how particular fences ride. Fences with alternative routes represent an added difficulty because although I have a rough idea of which competitors are more likely to ride the direct route and which ones are going to go the long way, one can never be sure! Ideally, I will try to secure an angle from which I can get a decent shot from the direct route and a good sequence from the alternative. I have learned over the years that gambling by only covering the direct route does not, unfortunately, always pay off!

Because competitors start at three- to five-minute intervals, getting from one fence to another between riders can also be tricky. Fortunately, photographers are allowed to walk inside the ropes of the course, which helps considerably because having to fight through the crowds at Badminton carrying two camera bodies, a minimum of three lenses (one of which is a 300 mm lens that weighs 2.5 kg) plus a monopod, spare batteries and film would considerably cut down your chances of getting to the next fence on time.

Just like the riders, I am also aiming to get through the day without any major hiccups! I cannot afford to miss any chances and have to trust my equipment fully. The rest is up to me. I have to be alert and get my timing right! Although I do feed off my adrenalin during the cross country, having to work all day without food or drink can be tiresome, especially when it's hot, but the last thing I want to

Jim Graham and Easter Parade, Althorp, 1994

do is carry yet another item. I am sure that if it wasn't for the generosity of some fence judges, who have offered me a drink, I would have collapsed in a heap once or twice!

In the following pages course designer Mike Etherington-Smith reveals the many aspects of his job.

Mike Etherington-Smith

Mike Etherington-Smith is one of the FEI's listed course designers which entitles him to design courses officially and to act as technical delgate at any three day event in the world. Mike has designed courses at most levels and has acted as the technical delegate at events on all five continents. In Britain he is probably best known for having taken Bramham from being a national three day event to its present international status before moving on to create the Audi International at Blenheim from scratch in 1990. In 1994 the Young Riders European Championships were held at Blenheim over Mike's course, alongside the existing CCI*** (Concours Complet International three star) competition. The American three day event in Lexington, Kentucky rates among the higher-profile courses Mike has designed. He also spends a lot of 'rewarding time, where ideas get kicked around' holding FEI clinics on cross country course designing. In 1995 Mike designed six cross country courses from scratch and is getting more and more involved in event management and consultancy.

Following in his father and grandfather's footsteps, Mike should have joined the navy but after inheriting £500 at the age of seventeen, which was spent on buying a horse and reselling it at a profit, Mike was inspired to take a different direction. He quickly bought another horse and it wasn't too long before he was eventing and jumping for other people while also taking his A levels. Plans to read French and business studies at university were soon set aside and Mike started his professional career with horses at Windmill Hill Riding Establishment, mainly producing youngsters and taking them up through the levels before they were sold. He considers himself lucky to have been given the chance to ride pretty good horses as well as some awful ones and regards this broad experience as a very useful asset in his course designing work. Although Mike did compete at Burghley once and Badminton twice in his mid-twenties, he began to realise that he was going to be neither 'a Toddy nor a hot shot in the eventing world … If you are a bloke you've either got to be exceptionally good or get out of it sensibly. I had a wife and two children and was very conscious about the fact that I didn't want to reach forty and still be competing!'

While Mike was still competing, the BHS Horse Trials Group heard that he wanted to leave the competition side of things and invited him to join them as a deputy advisor. In the late seventies and early eighties, Mike enjoyed giving advice on courses and also ran the occasional Pony Club Event, building their courses. However, the final decision to give up competing came in 1985 when Mike thought he went round Badminton 'riding like at Pony Club' and, although he completed, 'I didn't cover myself with glory either'. While he was a technical advisor he was asked to get more involved in the sport of eventing. The big leap into course designing came in 1987 when he was asked to raise the status of Bramham Three Day Event to international level. When Blenheim came on offer, the BHS asked Mike to do a feasibility study to see whether a three day event could, indeed, be held there. The answer was positive and Mike took on the task of designing the course as well as being the event's director.

A lot of work and thought goes into running and designing a course, beginning with a blank piece of paper. 'I start off by going to the ground and I spend as long as it takes to get a real feel for the place. Inevitably, the design of any course has to fit in with the structure of the event. You have to consider locations for the car park, the arenas, the horse box

park, the stables, and assess the general shape of the event. One of the main priorities is to make it user-friendly. Big events have to be spectator-friendly, television-friendly and, obviously, it's got to be competitor- and horse-friendly. You have got to think about how the people are going to walk around and whether they will be able to see enough.

'Then there is the major consideration in the

Blyth Tait, Vicky Latta and Mark Todd walking the cross country course at the Barcelona Olympics

form of the budget. I talk to organisers and find out what sort of event they are wanting. What their aims are and how much money they want to spend. Do they want to come up with the most spectacular event in one go or to have the event unfold over three to four years? Budget is very important because one thing you want to avoid is designing a fabulous course and then being told that you have overspent. The whole course is like a jigsaw, all fences relate to each other and you can't just cut out little bits because it has cost too much. In a course each fence has a reason for being there, and a series of fences is not a proper course in my book!

'I spend a lot of time just walking to establish a route, a line that flows around the course, something that, if you had no fences there, a rider could come out of the starting box and ride around in a very comfortable way. I use the existing features and if there is a shortage of them, you need to perhaps create some. If there is an abundance of features, you need to avoid the temptation to overuse them. The ground has to talk to you a little bit.

'I spend a lot of time watching horses cover the ground and how they cope physically with different types of fences on all sorts of ground. This gives me a better understanding of the type of fences that give horses a good feel, possibly what gives them a bad experience and therefore it tells me the things to avoid. If you walk and move around and look at the ground from different directions, you get totally different perspectives. I can move ten feet in one direction and suddenly I've got a different fence, so

most courses really design themselves. I have to be comfortable with the route and where the features are on the course. The finished product has to flow, have a good rhythm once a horse is put into the situation.

'The water is a major factor in governing the shape of a course. I don't want the water jump too early and if I have only one position for it, I need to build the course around it because it really wants to be somewhere in the middle of the course. For the start and finish I look at the ground and, in my experience, the last few obstacles are the most difficult to build. You have to keep the horse interested particularly in three day eventing. You don't do anyone any favours by producing small fences. Horses start getting tired, riders can easily underestimate small fences and press the go button, looking to get inside the time. I like to keep the horses concentrating. I avoid long periods between fences because it can cause horses to switch off, lose interest and become casual. Speed is also extremely important and I am very conscious of using certain types of fence to regulate the competitors' speed. I can slow down competitors without them really noticing it and we are all guilty of producing courses that ride too fast.'

When the design has been made, it is crucial to establish a good rapport with the actual builder of the course. 'I won't design a course and then walk away from it. I monitor and check the fence building a lot. The builder has to try and understand what I'm trying to design. In certain situations it can mean that we have to push and squeeze on the shape of a fence because of the terrain and it can result in throwing the measure tape away and getting the actual height and dimensions by eye.'

The ideology behind Mike's designing is very straightforward. 'My first aim is to educate horses and riders and I don't like producing what I consider

possible, I will give the rider the opportunity to make a mistake where the outcome would be a glance off rather than a fall. I know that, together with Mark Phillips, we have had a lot of stick in the past for producing arrowhead fences and maybe we did overdo it but, nevertheless, it got us away from

Samantha Bell and Solo II, Althorp, 1994

to be the ultimate test. In whatever I do, I try and come up with a test that, when the rider makes a mistake, will not penalise the horse. I don't like seeing horses punished through rider errors. I am not going to stop falls because you can ride a bike and have a fall and it's the same with a horse. As far as

the big straightforward fences. The standard of riding is so high now that big fences are not sufficient anymore when you are trying to sort out the good from the bad. The relationship between the fences has become the key for getting your result and sorting the well prepared horses from the not so well prepared ones. I always try to do that by seeing if riders can relate between obstacles, whether they understand when to just leave the horses alone, letting them run and jump. I do like the accurate fences; it's a very simple test where riders just have to ride straight, but not many can.'

When designing, Mike doesn't look at the field of riders who might take part. 'It's too late then and this is what makes course designing so exciting. I have to put my cards on the table before I know who's going to be there. I have to build to the

biggest challenge is getting the standard right. It is not so much about the dimensions of fences because we are governed by rules. It comes down to their shape, using particular fences in certain situations and in relation to others. It's what feels right and what doesn't.'

As with any form of art, creativity very much depends on the personal approach one chooses to finding inspiration. 'I can't design on a blank piece of paper; I've got to be on the ground. There are days when I go to a place and I have to walk away from it

**Myung-Jin Choi (Korea),
Althorp, 1994**

standard of the competition and it's the FEI that sets this on a global basis. There are various stages all the way up and I relate to that. After all, a one day event is part of the preparation for a three day event. The

because nothing happens. I find that, often, two or at the most three hours are enough before I have to leave it, have lunch or perhaps even walk away from it altogether and revisit another day. Once I have the

If I have a big ditch like fence five at Blenheim, I want to give the competitors a warm-up ditch before it so that they don't just come powering into the big one as the first ditch on the course. If I ask a series of three to four difficult questions, and by that I mean a fence where the horse is going to work hard, I always put a let-up fence afterwards to give the horse a chance to re-establish its confidence. I do this at every level. I'm very comfortable asking horses a question or two and then letting them settle back with an easy fence which can be a big straightforward galloping one. It is very easy to lose a horse's confidence and if you frighten a

Eric Smiley, Althorp, 1994

route mapped out, I'll start filling in the fences, and I know pretty well where the feature fence and the combinations will be because the land dictates that. You know that you will have to prepare your horses.

horse, you can set it back for as long as a year.

'I try to get the riders thinking because a horse has such a short time in which to evaluate a fence before doing what it's asked to do, and for me it must instantly and clearly understand the questions. There needs to be a definition to any type of fence enabling the horse to assess the situation. As soon as a horse gets frightened, the first thing it does is drop its legs. I don't want this to happen once it's airborne over a solid fence. I like to give the horse the opportunity to make up its mind whether it's going to jump something or not by knowing what the question is.'

Any horse, at whatever level, should be able to jump a straightforward fence of maximum dimensions. Nevertheless, there are situations where every course designer has to incorporate alternative routes. 'I will consider putting an alternative in where there is an element of severity to a fence that requires a bit more experience on the part of the rider or the horse. Most water jumps and corner fences will need an alternative. Sometimes I'll put in an alternative at a fence that I don't consider as being very difficult, simply to make the riders think, so there is a little psychology in it too. It is important to make any alternative fence flow because there is nothing worse than seeing riders hooking and pulling their horses going round the long route. At major championships where you have riders at many different levels, you need to look after the less experienced ones because you cannot afford to kick them out of the sport. They have got to come along and feel that they have the chance to be competitive. There are times when I put an alternative in to help a horse that might have had a bad experience at a previous fence. The next fence coming up could be a big one and a rider may very well see the alternative

as an opportunity to give their horse that little bit extra time to settle down and start feeling good again. For me the alternatives are really more for the horses than the riders. If the riders are not capable of jumping the types of fences that they are presented with then they shouldn't be at the competition in the first place.'

By the time cross country day comes along, the course designer will have put their signature on the course and all that remains now is for him or her to watch horses and riders tackle the questions that are confronting them. 'There is nothing I can do at this stage because I wouldn't put a course in front of people if I'm not comfortable with it myself. We all have our own method of how to assess and evaluate a course. Mine is whether I would be prepared to ride round it myself. As long as I'm comfortable with that, I'm not going to be nervous. I don't believe in worrying about things I don't have any control over and at that stage I have no control over it anymore. I always like to go to cross country control where the communications are coming in so that I know what is happening. I also want to see how the time is working; I don't like having too many finish inside the time. Then I'll go round the course and watch horses go over various fences and how they cover the ground. Afterwards I will watch the video so that I get to see which fences jumped well and those that didn't, viewing the latter ones over and over to try and figure out why they didn't jump well.'

Any UK course designer is also responsible for phases A, B, C and D of the speed and endurance,

Tiny Clapham and the then ten-year-old Kangaroo were pretty inexperienced as a partnership on their first big outing at Burghley in 1994. Time faults on the steeplechase and the cross country, as well as having two show jumps down, meant that they finished in nineteenth place.

'Kangaroo is a typical redhead! He's all full of bounce and a real tiger, there is nothing gentle in him. Kangaroo would never deviate; if you would ask him to jump a house, he would. He's got an unbelievable turn of foot, almost like a cat. He is very bold and we may be jumping ourselves into trouble at times but he is so sharp that he can assess any situation. This means that you have got to stay quite cool with him because if you think that you want to turn right, he will have turned right before you have even thought it. He is the most talented horse but has an unstable character which, to say the least, gives you the most thrilling rides!'

whereas in the United States he or she is asked to build the show jumping course as well. In Europe, however, their main tasks, other than designing the cross country course, are to ensure that the two roads and tracks as well as the steeplechase are properly set up. 'You need to understand the relationship between all four phases because they relate to each other. The distances I am asking on phases A and C are in relation to what I'm demanding on phases B and D. The second roads and tracks doesn't want to be too short because it's supposed to be a recovery period and the first roads and tracks needn't be terribly long. However, there are certain parameters within which they have to be set. The steeplechase can be designed how you want, right- or left-handed, or in a figure of eight but, again, it depends on how the ground lends itself. The steeplechase is not a test in its own right as far as the jumping is concerned. It's an exercise, seen as part of the speed and endurance, to test whether the horse can gallop for four to four and a half minutes before recovering on phase C and still be able to go on to phase D.'

When a course designer is asked to be technical delegate at a major championship, he will have been appointed by the FEI to represent them. At other three day events he still represents the FEI but will have been invited by the organiser. 'My first job would be to arrive on the Monday and inspect phases A, B, C and D, ahead of the ground jury. The technical delegate, the course designer and the organiser all work closely together and they have to make sure that the course that has been produced is at the right standard, fair and safe before they hand over the responsibility to the ground jury.'

Wearing his course designer cap, Mike likes to get feedback from riders once they have had a chance to reflect on their round objectively. 'I want to know whether courses I have designed gave them a good or bad feel but quite often you can tell by watching. If you look at a horse on the last quarter mile of a course and it has its ears pricked no matter how tired it is, quite often it will have had a good time. If horses are coming home head down and ears back you know that they have struggled. Talking to riders can be instructive but quite often the only thing they will think of is how to get their horse from one side of the fence to the other. The same fence can work well for one horse but not for another and it usually depends on how the rider has presented it to his horse.'

Like most designers, Mike would love to design for the Olympics or the World Championships. He believes that creating for that level is getting more interesting and will demand additional requirements now that it distinguishes between the team and the individual competitions. His ultimate aim, however, is 'to produce a good competition that is fair, safe and that does the sport proud'. Mike feels privileged to work in beautiful parks and enjoys being on his own surrounded by nature and wildlife. He is very passionate about his job and keen to emphasise the positive side of the sport. 'I want to give people the opportunity to show what they can do and how well they have trained their horses and I hope that it comes through in all the courses I design.'

Most teams used the 1994 Althorp Championship as their final selection for the World
Equestrian Games which followed a few weeks later. Hampshire-based Australian David Green
and the Thoroughbred Chatsby had put on a terrific performance across country.

'At that stage I was still supposed to ride Duncan at the World Championship and it wasn't
until I walked the course in The Hague that I decided to ride Chatsby instead because of the
heat. I thought that, being a full Thoroughbred, he would be more suitable. It proved to be the
right decision because he finished the course full of going. He has got a lot of jumping ability
and could just as well go pure show jumping, he's that careful over his fences. He is learning to
trust me now and getting a lot braver. He is one of the fastest horses I have ever sat on but he
will play up with you if you are not on top of him at all times. Chatsby is a bit of a rogue but
definitely a fun horse for the future'

In 1988 Ginny Elliot and Murphy Himself were one of the last combinations to tackle the infamous Normandy Bank at Badminton. This was memorable for Ginny not only because this fence was taken out of the course the following year but because Murphy dumped Ginny in a most spectacular way at the next fence, the Ski Jump. The result was pretty dramatic: Ginny broke her ankle and, after a family meeting, it was decided that the headstrong Murphy should be exchanged for Ian Stark's Griffin. Ginny had started Murphy off as a four year old and won Burghley, Le Touquet and Avenche with him.

'Murphy was a very aggressive four year old and whenever I tried to teach him a new movement, like shoulder-in or rein-back, he always, always, always did a sort of levade, landed, bucked and then stood still. I would try it again and he would do the same thing. I never ever used a stick on him, I just had to go through these moments of total aggression and then, suddenly, he would say "OK, fine" and he would do the movement and never be naughty again. He was just an incredibly brave horse. I loved him in spite of his aggressive character because I thought that he was just such a brilliant horse. I actually wanted to keep Murphy and I don't think a day has gone by in which I haven't regretted the decision to swap him with Griffin'

In 1993 Welton Houdini surprised Ginny Elliot by reaching his peak just for the occasion and helped her to win Badminton for the third time.

'I remember this moment at the lake very well. A look of grim determination! Welton Houdini did an enormous jump into the water. Within the first stride he had a little peck and I thought, "My God we are going to go straight out", so I let go of the left rein completely to get both hands on the right rein. He had locked his jaw and wasn't very keen on turning right. Luckily he did and we just about scraped our way through. Winning Badminton on Houdini was extra special. He had done a good dressage test but really it was only after fence four that I realised we were in with a squeak. He jumped brilliantly, so I put my foot down thinking that I had a good chance. Houdini has an incredibly generous nature. He's not very quick thinking but he would do his utmost to get over the fences as best he could'

Leslie Law ensured that Welton Envoy kept his concentration over the last fence at Althorp in 1994 and their determination was rewarded with the championship title. Although the pair had previously won Blarney Castle Three Day Event, this was only the third time Leslie had ridden him in an Advanced class. 'This was a big track for Welton Envoy. He had gone extremely well and I wasn't going to let it slip away at the last fence! He is very talented but yet extremely modest. He is really much better than he thinks he is so you have to constantly tell him that he is more than capable. He has a very reserved personality and always stands back to wait for someone to come up first to say hello. I have now sold my half share back to Sam Barr and the horse was supposed to be ridden by Jamie Atkinson in Juniors. He would have made a fabulous horse for a Junior but Sam then decided to let Charlotte Bathe ride him'

Robert Lemieux adopted
Canadian citizenship in 1991
and fulfilled an ambition to
represent his country at the
World Equestrian Games in
The Hague in 1994, riding the
then eight-year-old Kayem.
Halfway round the course the
pair took a ducking at the
water complex and retired.

'It was a shame because
Kayem was one of the
quickest horses up to
halfway. Although he can be
a little unorthodox at times,
jumping slightly higher
behind than in front, he has
a very good jumping
technique. He is probably one
of the best horses on the
circuit. Being a pure
Thoroughbred, he has great
stamina, almost the perfect
constitution and metabolism
for three day eventing. He
can be a bit spooky which
makes him a good show
jumper. He's quite arrogant
and calculating. He's always
very sure of himself and has
tremendous flair'

King Boris has been Mary King's faithful partner since he was a five year old and accompanied her all through her 'learning days'. In 1990 the pair came third at Badminton, one place lower than the previous year. They then went on to become national champions at Gatcombe the same year.

'I owe King Boris so much. He had to put up with a lot of my silly mistakes and helped me out of awkward situations more than once. He is such a genuine and forgiving horse that he would come out the next time and try his best again. He is not the most talented horse and finds galloping quite difficult but he's such a trier and I love him. He is so handsome and I could very easily picture him as a lifeguard at the beach, showing off his muscles to the girls'

King Kong fulfilled all of Mary King's dreams by coming second at his first four-star three day event at Burghley in 1994.

'It is very exciting when you get a young horse that you have produced right from the start up to that level. You always hope that they will be top class but it's not until you get to ask them the really big questions that you know. King Kong is terrific in all three phases. He shows enormous enthusiasm and boldness across country. His jumping has never been a problem, he's very tidy, focuses on his fences and bascules beautifully. His result at Burghley was very impressive and I think that he has also caught the selectors' eyes. I think if he continues showing such potential, he could be the one that will get to Atlanta'

After a thrilling cross country round on what was only Biko's second three-star three day event, US rider Karen O'Connor was delighted to find that the Irish-bred gelding had finished in sixth place.

'Biko is probably far and away the most talented horse in all three disciplines that I have ever ridden. I reckon that he could be a dressage horse or a show jumper if he wanted to. He has a great temperament although he was quite scared of people when he was young. For the first three years he needed someone at his head and someone on either side of him because he was just ready to tank off when I tried to get on him. I brought him along very slowly because he kept growing up until he was seven years old. He is seventeen-three hands now and he must be the smallest large horse and the biggest large horse I have ever ridden. He can take his size and, similar to an accordian, be like a pony, but he can also take his size and use it to his full advantage. This is an extraordinary sensation and an ability he came with. Biko gives you the feeling that there isn't anything you can't jump with him'

New Zealand event rider Victoria Latta and Chief came over to Europe to compete at the 1990 World Equestrian Games held in Stockholm. Their next flight home was scheduled for Febuary 1991 but, because of quarantine regulations, the pair would then have missed the season at both ends of the world which persuaded Vicky to base herself in Gloucestershire in England instead. Vicky and Chief have competed at Badminton every year since 1991. They came third in 1992, the same year that they narrowly missed the bronze medal at the Barcelona Olympics. In 1993 the pair went clear across country and finished fourth. 'Once I had decided to stay in Europe and, having had a good ride on Chief in Stockholm, I thought of entering him for Badminton. But after I had a look at the course I wondered why on earth I had done it! Chief is a tremendous horse. He has a strong personality with a mind of his own. He can be quite stubborn and dogmatic about things but at the same time he is very generous if he trusts you. I bought Chief from a friend of mine after he had been stopping with her. When trying him out I had to ring her to ask her what aid she used for the canter? It was obviously different to the aids I used! Chief has a very strong sense of justice. If he thinks that he's entitled to stop because you came in wrong and you hit him, he'll launch into orbit. I managed to get his confidence back by throwing the reins at him. This is where I got into the habit of riding him on such a long loose rein'

William Fox-Pitt and Chaka came second at the 1994 British Open Championship which is traditionally held on Mark Phillips's demanding course round Gatcombe Park.

'It was very exciting to ride a horse as good as Chaka round a course as testing as Gatcombe. To have a horse that can cope with the jumps and the terrain as well as Chaka did is very rare. I often used the event as a preparatory run for another event but in 1994 I really wanted to be in the competition, giving it my best shot. It was great fun to see Chaka handling it so well. He is a very good judge of a fence. He is very accurate, very careful and on the right day he's a big trier'

William Fox-Pitt and Chaka
had been partners for two
and a half years before
coming to Burghley in 1994
and clinching the famous
Rémy Martin trophy.

'Chaka is an exceptional
horse in as far as he does all
three disciplines extremely
well. He is fantastic across
country. OK, he's made
mistakes in the past and
people have criticised him
and he's had a few setbacks
in his youth which have made
him slightly cautious but I
prefer that, at least you
know that he's safe! At
Burghley he was as fit as he
could possibly be without
being unmanageable. He was
firing on all cylinders. I could
just feel that he came to
Burghley wanting to do well.
On the cross country he just
went out of his way to do his
best, whereas sometimes he
can go out of his way to be
unhelpful'

In 1990 US rider Mike Huber went round Badminton on his home-bred Thoroughbred Phoenix for the second year running. Finishing in tenth place in 1989, the pair had already proved themselves and knew that a clear round this time would secure them a spot on the US team for the Stockholm World Equestrian Games. They reached their goal when they became members of the US team and just missed out on a medal, finishing in fourth place. Although Mike was also a member of the US squad in 1994, he is probably best known for winning the 1987 Pan American Championship both with the team and as an individual.

'Badminton is certainly an imposing course and I was delighted with the way Phoenix went. It is a fabulous experience and I believe that from all the events in which I have participated, including world championships, it's still the best competition. Phoenix was extremely brave, a real cross country machine, highly strung and spooky, but once he was on the course he was all there. When Phoenix set off on the cross country, it didn't matter where you were and what course you were on. I always knew that he could jump a clear round and that we had the opportunity to stay inside the time. He was a tough and extremely fast individual, a real tiger. Phoenix was one of my mother's home-bred Thoroughbreds, so as far as choosing him was concerned she just gave him to me so I guess I would have ridden him eventually! Sadly, he had a freak accident and had to be put down'

Carolyne Ryan-Bell had actually qualified Hooray Henry four times for Badminton but, unfortunately, something always prevented them from competing. In 1994 she had finally realised her dream and the pair finished in sixteenth place. Carolyne considers herself a professional amateur as she has brought Hooray Henry up through the ranks but has always had to work to support her hobby.

'I have always been competitive at heart and I thrive on challenge. I went the direct route at the Vicarage Vee and I believe it's one of the hardest fences on the course because of the big ditch. You have got to be so accurate. In 1994 we had to jump the bridge before and if you do a big jump over that and it feels good, it sets you up for the Vicarage Vee and you know that you'll be all right. Hooray Henry almost goes into computer mode after a few fences and, as long as I am right, I just aim and don't mess around too much. Although he's very quick footed and terribly clever, he'll jump anything apart from water. I can always rely on him as long I am with him. If I fell off, he'd wait for me and wonder what I was doing back there'

Australian Matt Ryan and Kibah Tic Toc survive a tricky moment during the cross country on their way to winning the individual and team gold medals at the 1992 Barcelona Olympics.

'When I was in the ten-minute box, I heard that this fence was causing a few stops so, as I came round the corner and down the hill, I really drove Tic Toc very hard. It was quite a spooky-looking fence, so I cantered strongly into it to compensate should the horse back off. Because I was coming in so fast, I didn't see my distance well enough and I was a little bit too far off. Tic Toc decided that the stand-off stride I asked him for was just too far away and he chipped in another little stride. It felt very uncomfortable and all I could do was to try and sit as tight as possible. Tic Toc threw me up very high and I tried to restrict him as little as I could with my hands and stay as balanced as possible. He gave me a bit of a fright and continuing down the hill over the hanging log I gave him a few slaps to tell him not to frighten me like that again! The cross country is really Tic Toc's best phase; he's got a relentless gallop. He is not speedy at one day events but he's great at three day events. He is very bold, you just point him on a line diagonally across a fence over a ditch and he will stick to it'

Despite 'a stupid stop' at the first fence of the Luckington Lane Crossing, Australian Matt Ryan and Kibah Tic Toc cruised round the 1994 Badminton course within the time, finishing in twelfth place.

'There is no doubt that riding at Badminton is a wonderful thrill but I can also tell you that whenever I start a big cross country course, I'm scared. I get incredibly nervous and sometimes even physically sick in the ten-minute box. When I get scared, I sometimes wonder why the hell I'm doing it? The great thrill is finishing; it gives you a real high. Your adrenalin is running, you're very excited and when it's going quite well, particularly at an event of the magnitude of Badminton, I feel exhilarated, relieved and at the same time almost glad that it's over. I have always got to psych myself up into doing the job. At the start I will growl at myself, sometimes give Tic Toc a slap on the shoulder, which is more for me but also to tell him that I'm aggressive and ready to go. You can never go round a cross country course tentative. It's very important for your own safety to be aggressive. That doesn't mean wild nor crazy fast but certainly positive'

The New Zealand rider Blyth Tait and Messiah were relatively inexperienced when they
competed at the 1990 Stockholm World Equestrian Games. A chance of a 'second life' at the
water complex, where Messiah was just 'a bit too enthusiastic', was the only sticky moment
the pair had to overcome on their way to victory.

'The course in Stockholm really suited Messiah because it was twisty and he's quick on his
feet, very agile and athletic. It had been the biggest track Messiah had encountered until then
but he was certainly at his peak of fitness and, having had a confident preparation, he handled
it well. Messiah is definitely quite hot-headed. He does everything with a hustle and a bustle.
He is a horse that has the utmost confidence in his ability. He would assess and sum up a
situation across country as quick as a flash'

Tempo found his way into Blyth Tait's yard with a view to being sold on. In 1994 the two had been through all the preparation, pressure and tension that is involved with getting to Badminton but failed the trot up on the final day.

'Badminton is definitely the one event everybody wants to win! The course is as big and demanding as you can get. Every fence asks a question so you really have to keep your wits about you at all times and keep attacking. Tempo is a horse that, unfortunately, missed the boat! Whenever he performed exceptionally well and got it all right on the day, he would have soundness problems. He is a horse that never really fulfilled his potential. The sad thing is that his lameness was always minor, of a different nature each time and he was usually fine a few days later. He was a slightly quirky horse that could lose his concentration very easily'

After having caught the selectors' eyes with a thirteenth place at Badminton, Caroline Sizer and Ghost Town underlined their form at the 1994 Althorp Championship by finishing in sixteenth place which earned them a place as an individual combination at the 1994 World Equestrian Games. There, Caroline experienced her biggest disappointment to date. The heat and humidity affected Ghost Town to the extent that the pair were held at the ten-minute box and not allowed to carry on.

'Ghost Town loves the cross country. In one day events the dressage can be a problem because as soon as he hears the tannoy and horses being started on the course, he wants to be part of the action. He really lives for the cross country. He is usually very easy to ride across country because he is always looking where he is going. He wants to get over the fences rather than trying to get out of his job. He is very cocky and thinks that he is just too cool. Ghost Town is my best friend. My husband says that I think more of Ghost Town than I do of him, which doesn't go down too well! So I tell him that it's because I have known him for only five years and I've known Ghost Town for almost fifteen'

When competing at Althorp in 1994, double World Champion
Bruce Davidson (1974 at Burghley on Irish Cap and 1978 in
Lexington on Might Tango) wasn't looking for a spot in the
US team in these pre-World Equestrian Games selection
trials. Previously, the pair had won a three-star in the US, as
well as being placed fourth, both at Badminton in 1994 and
at Burghley in 1993.

'Eagle Lion jumped the course at Althorp beautifully. I
didn't go very fast across country and was just doing it as
an exercise. Eagle Lion has lots of personality, self-
confidence and self-expression. He is a marvellous horse to
ride at jumps and a marvellous galloper. He is quite the
opposite of a serious horse, life is very easy and full of jokes
for him and I feel that he has never really been challenged
yet, everything comes so natural to him. Eagle Lion is a true
athlete who jumps for joy and considers a day of jumping as
a day off'

Riding at Burghley brings back a realm of fond memories for US rider Bruce Davidson for he became World Champion here at the beginning of his career in 1974 on Irish Cap. In 1994 he rode the young and fairly inexperienced Regent Lion but withdrew him before the show jumping.

'Riding at Burghley is a wonderful experience. The terrain is challenging, the hills very long. They give a good pull on the horse and offer an indication as to how good an endurance horse you're really sitting on. Regent Lion jumped a little green but very brave. He gave me a good ride, overjumped at a couple of places which is a nice fault. But at the end of the day, Burghley made Regent Lion into a much bigger, grander and more capable animal. By the time he finished, he knew so much more about this game and about himself. Regent is a true gentleman, a very dashing-looking, intelligent individual. He is a tremendous workman and just likes to do his job properly. He loves to know that he is doing what you want him to do. You don't get very many horses that give you one hundred and ten per cent all the time. Regent Lion, however, just loves to oblige'

The then ten-year-old Irish Thoroughbred gelding Eagle Lion helped US rider Bruce Davidson to add the prestigious Badminton Trophy to his tally of international successes.

'I love producing young horses, it's real fun. When I was in the starting box, being counted down from ten, recollections of the first day I sat on Eagle Lion and how quickly he bucked me off and the first time I jumped him went through my mind. I was thinking, "You little bugger, it was only five years ago that you were putting me on the floor, spinning around and here you are about to challenge Badminton," and he did it so well! Eagle Lion loves jumping, for him it comes right after breakfast, lunch and dinner. Winning here was just a matter of me staying focused on his job and not making any mistakes. I knew he'd bring me home, he always has! I did my job and just let the chips fall where they were going to fall'

New Zealand rider Vaughn Jefferis and Bounce travelled to England to prepare for the World Equestrian Games that were to be staged in The Hague later in the season, and scheduled Badminton into their programme for the run up to the games. Although Bounce had come to Badminton after only two outings due to a bad virus, Vaughn felt pretty confident of his horse's courage, knowing that he had the right preparation before leaving his home country. Coming third behind fellow countrymen Mark Todd and Blyth Tait confirmed just that. 'Bounce is quite a cautious horse by nature and a very careful jumper. With that combination in an event horse people would normally steer clear because they may feel that he might have too much self-preservation to be brave enough. But I also knew that he has a big heart and I knew that with a lot of careful preparation, never running him unless he was right and that by taking my time with him, I was going to have something pretty special in Bounce. He is always very cautious when jumping into water and needs to have a good look. Originally, I used to be quite spooked by it, thinking that he would stop. But I know him really well now and let him look and feed him the reins because he wants to know where his legs are at, only then does he jump at his best'

Lorna Clarke is certainly one of the most accomplished three day event riders in Britain. Her unbeaten track record of completing Badminton 23 times speaks for itself. In 1990 she had an unlucky fall on Fearliath Mor and the pair finished in thirty-ninth place. Although the horse was 'dogged with bad luck' when it came to championships or Olympic Games, they won an individual bronze and a team gold medal at the 1989 European Championships where they started as pathfinders for the team, scoring a superb clear round across country as well as in the show jumping.

'Riding at Badminton is like banging your head against a brick wall; it's so wonderful when you stop! It's also like a drug. You dread it, but you can't do without it so you keep coming back! When you get there, you think why the hell did I come back? Yet if your horse goes lame or someone says you can't go, you'd go bananas. Fearliath Mor is probably one of the most brilliant horses I have ever ridden across country. He was great for me as I was getting older because his one aim was to get over to the other side, fighting what was in front of him without touching it. He didn't like any discipline and I think that if you would have broken his spirit and put him under your thumb, he wouldn't have been any good. He was an ugly little runt that stepped out of his class but I am devoted to him because he is so brave and was such a brilliant horse to me'

After having won a team bronze medal on Kildare at the 1992 Barcelona Olympics, German rider Ralf Ehrenbrink decided to ask his national trainer if he could ride Kildare at the 1993 Badminton Horse Trials. His wish was granted and, apart from having a run out at the Beaufort Staircase, for which Ralf blames himself, the pair had an enjoyable time, finishing in twenty-fourth place after a faultless show jumping round.
'I am always extremely happy when I am allowed to compete at Badminton because it simply represents the ultimate test for us Germans. Kildare jumped superbly, especially when tackling the direct way at the lake complex where he kept his line perfectly. He is not a horse that can be forced into anything. He does have a mind of his own and ultimately always does what he thinks is best. He also has the ability to find a fifth leg in situations where other horses are practically sure to fall. He is such a clever horse, always thinking, and I am convinced that he is able to read and write! I would like to retire him after the German National Championships at the end of 1996 and the nicest gift would be if he could end his career feeling healthy and well'

US rider David O'Connor and the Irish gelding On A Mission didn't have 'a fun time' round the cross country course at the 1994 World Equestrian Games. Although the pair completed the three days, On A Mission never really got into his usual rhythm and had two uncharacteristic stops on the way. David is convinced that the heavy sand on the roads and tracks 'tore the horse's ankle apart' which explains why On A Mission went lame a few days after the end of the competition. The injury meant that the horse was out for a year and only started work again in June 1995. The pair have, however, a great track record, never being placed lower than fourth, apart from Burghley 1993 when they missed a corner.

'On A Mission has the tendency to be very aggressive in his last couple of strides. At this fence he got way up underneath it and had to do everything possible to get out of trouble. It was the perfectly wrong course for him with all those twisty little turns where you would expect to leave him alone to figure out the ropes. With hindsight I am sure that he ran a little hurt which is why he went badly but it actually also shows what a gutsy horse he is. He is a bit of a Dr Jekyll and Mr Hyde type because he can be very laid back and then suddenly he can get quite difficult to ride. He dumps me at least two to three times a year, wheeling out underneath me. He can be wonderful and suddenly turn into a wild animal'

French rider Marie-Christine Duroy and Quart Du Placineau, owned by the French National Stud, finished sixth at their first attempt round Badminton in 1993. The pair also finished Burghley in sixth place the year before and represented their country at the 1992 Barcelona Olympics.

'I have always had the desire to ride at Badminton but it is very difficult for us French to convince our federation and the national trainer to be allowed to take our best horses to Badminton as they feel that we shouldn't risk them here but, instead, should be saving them for major championships. I have visited as a spectator at least ten times and always told my husband that I would ride here one year. He never believed me but, finally, with the appointment of a new national trainer, I got permission. Quart Du Placineau jumped clear but I feel that I let him down because everybody told me that I couldn't win Badminton at my first attempt and that the first year should be treated as a discovery round and I should be prepared to encounter problems. I believed too much in what I had been told and rode slightly on the defensive, waiting for something to happen. It was only six fences from home that I thought, "To hell with all these voices, just go for it." But it was too late and I was twenty seconds over the optimum time. I am not saying that I could have won, but I could have had a better placing. A win at Badminton would be a tremendous boost and would help re-evaluate eventing in France in relation to show jumping. I love all three disciplines although I definitely favour the cross country phase. This doesn't mean to say that I am not terrified when I am in the ten-minute box but once I'm off I am fully concentrated and when I reach the finishing line I want to be off again!'

Flying Scotsman Ian Stark and Sir Wattie won Badminton for the first time in 1986 when this type of fence, known as The Huntsman's Hangover, was first introduced. The pair repeated their win in 1988 and went on to secure an individual as well as a team silver medal at the Seoul Olympics.

'We were all terrified that we were going to get our heads knocked off. I don't think that it affected the horses, they all jumped it very well, but it was a big fence at the end of the course. Wattie was as honest as the day was long. He used to keep jumping and pegging along but he got pretty tired in 1986 in that deep mud. No matter how tired he was, he would never make a mistake. From the first day I rode Wattie I believed that he was something special. He wasn't as talented as Murphy Himself or Glenburnie, he didn't have the speed nor the scope, but he was just an out and out winner. He was the most genuine horse, gutsy, very determined and a saint. He will always be my all-time favourite'

Ian Stark represented Great Britain for the third time running at the 1992 Barcelona Olympic Games. There he partnered Murphy Himself and a nasty knock coming out of the second water complex resulted in Murphy not passing the final veterinary inspection. The blow was deeply felt, especially as the British team was lying in silver medal position after the cross country, but with Murphy gone the team simply crumbled.

'Murphy gave me a really good ride across country. The only fence that terrified me was the drop into the first water. Murphy bounced it so well that we were both a bit blasé by the time we got to the second water and nearly met our Waterloo! Murphy hit the fence hard. Ninety-nine per cent of horses would have fallen but because he was such a strong horse he kept his feet and shook it off. He had also suffered from the heat and didn't feel great the next morning. The ground jury were right to kick him out but when you get to that stage and you've got the team and everyone else, not to mention the whole country, relying on you, it is difficult to turn round and not present your horse. I gave it a go but it wasn't meant to be. I felt completely gutted. At that moment the disappointment felt like it was the end of the world!

Murphy was probably the most talented event horse ever but his talent almost got in his way a lot of the time. When I first took over the ride from Ginny I hated him. I thought that he didn't feel at all like the horse I had seen Ginny win Burghley on! I couldn't relate what I was feeling to what I had seen. But I soon loved to ride him; I just had to learn to trust him. One simply couldn't interfere with him and the only time I did, I fell off him. I did develop a lot of faith in him and our relationship was pretty exhilarating. He was like an absent-minded professor with the body of Arnold Schwarzenegger'

Ian Stark reckons that Murphy Himself had given him the most brilliant ride ever when the pair sailed round the course at the 1991 Badminton Horse Trials. Ian still believes that Murphy was robbed of the title by having a show jumping fence down and although they took second place, he regards Murphy as having won it.

'In 1990, when I was told at the World Equestrian Games to ride a fast round, I got criticised by Captain Mark Phillips for riding a slightly hairy round. At the time I was pretty cheesed off by his criticism so the next spring I brought Murphy out, changed his bit to a cherry roller American gag and decided that, instead of riding him in a slow canter to try and keep him in control, I would work him at a faster cross country pace. It worked and I had the most fantastic feeling of power, scope and ability but in control. He listened, mind you he still bounced the bottom of the Beaufort Staircase, but there was no moment where I gasped or thought that he did something that he shouldn't have done. I don't suppose that I will ever again ride a horse of his scope and ability'

The Irish Thoroughbred Overdrive had been in Mark Barry's yard since he was a foal and was actually bred to go racing but, because he ended up missing the sales, the family decided to take him eventing. The pair took on the Seniors when Mark was still a Junior and impressed with a thirteenth place at the 1993 European Championships in Achselschwang. They went on to finish in eighth place at Burghley in 1994. At Badminton in 1993 they suffered the disappointment of not getting to the final trot up when lying fifteenth after the cross country.

'It was one of those things. Overdrive had jumped a very clean round and I couldn't tell you where he knocked himself. He was an exceptional jumper and very fast with it. He always made a nice shape over a fence. You could be coming very quiet and deep to a fence and he would really open up over it. The atmosphere at Badminton is almost like in the parade ring at the Gold Cup. You've got to work hard to relax there! It's also a bit like out hunting. Although you will have walked the course three times and picked out your line, there is so much around you on the day that you just gallop down to the fences and jump them as they come up. The biggest ambition for me would be to produce a good show at the 1998 World Equestrian Games in Punchestown in front of my home crowd'

Australian National Champion of 1991, Daniel Wilson spent some time with Ian Stark and then with Lord and Lady Vestey before taking Capitano to their first Badminton in 1994. The then only eight-year-old pony-Thoroughbred-cross cleared all the fences but incurred twenty penalties for a technical refusal in the lake when the pair left the penalty zone and had to cross their tracks before jumping out. They finished twentieth and received the Glentrool Trophy for being the horse and rider whose final position showed the greatest improvement from their dressage placing.

'It was a hell of a buzz to ride a three day event of that calibre. Capitano jumped terribly well; he is an incredibly athletic horse and it was a great honour to ride him at such an event. He is a very quick-thinking horse who can get himself out of any situation you put him in. Capitano is a bit of a troublemaker but he likes to get on with things. He is not a horse that wants to be mollycoddled; he likes to do his job and then be left alone for the rest of the day, preferably out in the field. He can be very boisterous and big-headed but he has lots of confidence when he is on the job. He can jump a seriously big fence and has an amazing talent for his size – he's only sixteen-one. I would describe him as a hot-headed little animal with a lot of ability'

Karen Dixon and Get Smart never failed to be well placed at Badminton. They have been clear and within the time every year apart from 1992 when they were a fraction over the optimum time. They have competed at two consecutive Olympic Games, two World Championships and three European Championships. In 1993 Get Smart attacked the big logs leading into the Badminton lake brilliantly, cruising through the water complex with ease.

'Badminton is the "crème de la crème" of three day eventing, something we all want to win. As far as ambitions go, it comes right after wanting to win Olympic gold. Get Smart is a fantastic cross country horse, he can gallop and jump forever no matter whether the conditions are hot or cold, which was his great asset during the Olympics and The Hague. He is a wonderfully bold jumper. He can be naughty, especially in the dressage at Badminton when he can still squeal and buck in spite of being worked for four and a half hours beforehand!'

Karen Dixon considers Get Smart's achievements at The Hague, where the pair won individual bronze and team gold at the 1994 World Equestrian Games, as his best results.

'Get Smart was on great form before the games. He felt really good and, on cross country day, ready to run for his life. He also did one of his best dressage tests ever. The ground on the roads and tracks was horrendous and really tired the horses. Luckily, Get Smart didn't feel too bad and, after a bit of recovery in the ten-minute box, he just went brilliantly. I knew that he could run in heat, so I simply put my foot down. In the show jumping he had the last fence down which was really unfortunate but, in fact, it was better for me because had he stayed clear I would have missed the individual gold medal by 0.2 points and I think I would have probably died!'

Karen Dixon and the then eight year old Too Smart came to the 1994 Burghley Rémy Martin Horse Trials as the reigning national champions, a title they had acquired at the British Open Championships at Gatcombe Park only a few weeks earlier. They had also won Punchestown Three Day Event in the spring of the same year. Finishing third at Burghley proved that the pair were still riding on the crest of a wave. Coming into the Upper Trout Hatchery certainly confirmed that they meant business.

'Too Smart was very strong at the beginning of the course and I was hoping that the fence before was going to slow him up because I couldn't hold him at that stage. I came into the water completely out of control. Being the bold and brilliant jumper he is, I didn't have a shadow of a doubt about his ability coming into the water. I knew that if he had been in trouble he would have just taken it at the trot. "Barrel" has me completely figured out; he is so bossy round the cross country. He gets on with it, makes all the arrangements and I just hang in there!'

Kristina Gifford and Song And Dance Man have formed a successful partnership since their Pony Club days. Winning a team gold medal at the 1987 Junior European Championships, a team silver at the Young Riders European Championship in 1989 and a European Championship individual silver medal at senior level rank among their greatest accomplishments. They have been round Badminton twice, finishing tenth in 1992 and fourteenth the following year.

'Song And Dance Man is a little Thoroughbred with a heart of gold. He will try to jump whatever you are pointing him at; he's very quick and sharp. I remember seeing quite a good stride to the Vicarage Vee and the way he jumped just shows you how much scope he could pull out over a fence as big as that. He is an absolute madman, a nutter really! He can be very difficult and doesn't enjoy his dressage. You can't school him much at home because he simply refuses. On the cross country he is like a little tiger, he will always give his best, but he can give a fair old pull too!'

Prairie King had only been round two three day events before Bermudian rider Nikki Parnell took him to the 1992 Barcelona Olympics. It was there that Nikki had the misfortune to come down with gastroenteritis the evening before the cross country. However, the then nine-year-old French-bred gelding really took care of Nikki. Apart from receiving ten penalty points for a technical error at the last water complex, which, incidentally, Prairie King shared with eleven other horses, including Vikki Latta's Chief who lost the bronze medal because of it, Nikki credits him with a clear round. The pair finished their three days in forty-fifth place.

'Everybody thought that it was nerves when I was taken ill because it started on the night before the cross country. I was cold and shivering, had a fever and felt really awful the following morning, rushing backwards and forwards to the toilet. I was in two minds whether I should compete but I was at the Olympics and one just has to go! Prairie King was brilliant, he just went round on auto-pilot! When I got off, I collapsed and the British doctor had to come over and see to me. Prairie King has a fantastic, quick-thinking brain and gives me great confidence. He also has a great sense of self-preservation and his scope will always get us out of a tight spot. Prairie King has an extra special space in the yard and in my heart; he means the world to me. After I got married, I went straight into the yard in my wedding dress and had my picture taken with him. The first picture in my photo album is of him and not of my husband and me!'

In 1994 Kristina Gifford took General Jock to his first Badminton. Because of the horse's inexperience, all Tina had in mind was 'to have a clear round and complete the competition' but, thanks to General Jock's great potential, he finished up seventh which earned him his ticket to the World Equestrian Games alongside his stable mate Song And Dance Man.

'Riding at Badminton means the world to me. It's a most amazing feeling, even when you are just walking around and not competing. Finishing the course inside the optimum time is a very special moment; you almost feel like crying. It's a relief as well because of the months of pressure and preparation beforehand. The whole year builds up to Badminton and once you have finished you are planning to get back there for next year'

Kristina Gifford travelled to the 1994 World Equestrian Games with the luxury of being able to choose between the two horses she had qualified, General Jock and Song And Dance Man. After having walked the course she decided to opt for General Jock, the younger one of the two. The decision proved to be right, the pair were members of the all-girl gold-medal-winning team. Jumping the second water complex, Tina was delighted with Jock's effort and gave him a big pat as they made their way through it.

'I felt that this was one of the most difficult fences on the course especially for Jock as he had never really jumped anything like it before. I was worried coming down to the bottom of the hill; seeing the lake gave me a horrible sinking feeling. I was just thinking that I had to keep my rhythm to it. I didn't see much of a stride until about the last two and he jumped it so well! Patting my horses when riding round the course is something I picked up from Lucinda Green. I feel that they appreciate a pat and understand it because it's something I do in

training. I will reward them when they do something right but I'm also very strict when they are naughty. So because they know that a pat is a reward, I'm sure that if they go across country and have jumped a fence that has made them think, or they have been very generous over it and have helped you out, it's only fair to let them know. If I have time or there is a stretch of field before the next fence, I will always do it. It only takes a minute and can mean so much to the horse! They should feel the partnership. Being a Thoroughbred General Jock is quite sensitive, he has a lot of ability. His achievements at the World Equestrian Games came so unexpectedly and I still think that there is a lot more to come from him'

British-based New Zealander Andrew Nicholson took Schiroubles to his first Badminton in 1990.
They completed the course despite a couple of stops towards the end. When South African rider
David Rissik needed a horse for the 1992 Barcelona Olympics, Andrew sold him Schiroubles. The
horse 'had the quality' and took the only South African competitor to thirtieth place.

   'Schiroubles was very easy to jump but he could tire mentally just as easily, which is why he
stopped at Badminton. He would also hype himself up, his adrenalin would run high the whole
week. He was a real athlete but very difficult to train. Competing at Badminton is very exciting
stuff when you're riding a good horse, but if you have a bad ride it's extremely nerve racking!
The atmosphere is rather serious which does rub off and can get you very uptight but you have
to try and enjoy what you are doing as well as taking it seriously'

Swedish rider Anna Hermann came to England in 1988 with
the plan of staying for a season to learn more about eventing.
Because she felt that she did not achieve what she wanted to
do in six months she is still here, operating out of Wiltshire
where she rents part of David Green's yard. Together with
Elektra Spiritus she won Boekelo in 1991 and finished
Burghley in sixth position in 1993. Here the pair are tackling
the lake at the 1994 Mitsubishi Motors Badminton Horse
Trials. Although they were lying eighth after the cross country,
Elektra Spiritus didn't pass the final veterinary inspection due
to a bruised sole after losing a shoe on the course.

'It's lovely the way Elektra Spiritus is just aiming at the
fence, ears pricked and eyes well focused on the fence. She
gave me an absolutely lovely feeling coming through the lake!
She is one of those horses that really trusts her rider and
listens, which, in return, makes me trust her. The nicest thing
about Elektra is that she really loves life. She can be quite a
nervy mare and you have to talk the same language to her.
Rather than dominate her you have always got to be prepared
to come to some sort of compromise. I know her so well now
and I am sure that she would never let me down'

Anna Hermann and the Irish bred Malacky have been a team ever since she broke him in. She then decided to buy him as a six year old. The purchase turned out to be quite dramatic because, had she not bought Malacky a week before her horse Unique died, Anna would have been left without a horse and believes that she probably would have given up the sport. As it turned out, Malacky gave Anna a good reason to carry on and the two went on to win Saumur in 1992 before representing Sweden at the Barcelona Olympics where they finished in forty-third place.

'I remember our fall at the water only too well! It was really silly! However, I think that Malacky is the best horse I have got, he can jump, moves extremely well and can really gallop. Unfortunately, he has been sidelined with sarcoid problems for the best part of two years. He is a real gentleman and the kindest horse. He was brought up on a bottle because his mother died when he was a foal, which has almost turned him into a person. He talks to you and follows you everywhere!'

After becoming German National Champion on Sundance Kid in 1993 at Luhmühlen, Marina Loheit decided to take her winning mount to their first Badminton Horse Trials the following spring. In the lead after the dressage, the pair had an unfortunate fall at the Second Luckington Lane Crossing and Marina decided to retire. In her last year as a young rider she became national champion and helped the team to a gold medal at the European Young Riders Championships. In this picture they are at the halfway marker and met the out fence of the lake complex beautifully.

'I still don't really know what happened at Luckington Lane. Sundance Kid just knuckled over on landing and we fell. Although he wasn't lame, I noticed that he had hurt his front fetlock so I wasn't going to risk him and felt that it was wiser to retire. Nevertheless, I still have fond memories of Badminton, it's a great place and I sincerely hope to come back some day. Competing at Badminton is a definite goal I set myself and I believe that if one has a horse capable of jumping the course,  especially if it has gone well during the previous season, one should give the horse the chance to prove itself at Badminton. The only problem for us Germans is that Badminton is a bit early in the season as we would have had only two starts beforehand whereas the British will have more opportunities to prepare their horses for it. Sundance Kid is a funny, mischievous boy; he can be really cheeky but extremely sweet too. He has a lot of talents, especially his jumping ability and the skill to know when he really has to pull himself together. He is unbelievably clever'

The Austrian three day event team, comprising three riders, fell apart when Peter Wagner was disqualified for leaving out a flag on the cross country course at the 1990 Stockholm World Equestrian Games. Harald Riedl and the then sixteen-year-old English Thoroughbred Jolly Jumper completed with a clear round across country and had one fence down in the show jumping, finishing in thirtieth place. Harald was Austrian Champion in 1982 and 1986 and qualified Jolly Jumper for the games by going clear across country at Luhmühlen in Germany a few months earlier. In Stockholm he had his fair share of excitement when he was close to being disqualified for entering the dressage arena wearing plastic spurs which had been banned by the FEI only a month before the competition. 'Jolly Jumper and I had totally lost our concentration due to this confusion and it was only thanks to Ian Stark, who spontaneously took off his spurs to hand them to me, that I was able to ride. Unfortunately, it was a rather disastrous test that put us well down the line but, mercifully, kept us in the competition. Jolly was fantastic across country, we jumped the direct route at the water as if it was a gymnastic exercise! He originally came to me via Germany where he had been written off as too difficult to handle. He had his problems at first but somehow we developed a marvellous partnership fairly quickly.

There was such substance to him; he had a relentless gallop and he never fell or stopped with me in his entire career. We were in real harmony and shared a mutual trust. He only had to wiggle his ears and I knew what he was about to do but I had to give him enough leeway. You couldn't try and place him at his fences. If he wanted to take off a stride too soon, I trusted him for knowing that he could get us over to the other side safely. After the championships I received a phone call from an English lady who recognised the horse on television. She had previously owned him in England when he was called White Snippers but had sold him on because he was too difficult. I am glad to say that we had a magic bond, the more testing the course, the better Jolly jumped'

The German Equestrian Federation followed their national trainer Horst Karsten's advice and bought the English Thoroughbred Watermill Stream for Bettina Overesch-Böker the year before they competed at the 1994 World Equestrian Games. As members of the German squad, the pair played an influential part in securing the team's bronze medal by jumping a clear round both across country and in the show jumping phase. Although they had a heart-stopping moment at the second water by almost coming to grief, an instant reaction and sheer willpower from both of them helped to overcome what could have ended in a ducking. The pair's determination was also rewarded with a seventh place in the individual classification.

'Watermill Stream lost a shoe jumping into the water and knuckled over on landing but, luckily, he lifted his head immediately and threw me back into the saddle and so on we went. This is also something I learned right from the start, to try and sit up and close your legs as soon as you can and Watermill Stream is great because, as soon as I put my leg on him, he's right there for me. Although I didn't know him for very long, I trust him implicitly on the cross country because he really pays attention especially at hairy moments like that. He manages difficult situations almost effortlessly and has a relentless and unconditional ambition. Although he was raced over fences as a youngster, he really respects the cross country obstacles. He truly looks after both of us but he isn't an easy horse, one couldn't just put anybody on him. He had his problems when I first got him, he was extremely distrustful and he still gets frightened, turns round and runs a mile which is why his stable name is "Spooky". I'd say he's a horse that you need a comprehensive manual for!'

While in the ten-minute box, anchor rider for Germany, Herbert Blöcker received strict orders from both the team trainer and the Chef d'Equipe to take the Holsteiner mare Feine Dame through all the direct routes on the cross country as 'a safe clear round would not have been good enough' if the team was to stay in the running for a medal. Following instructions, Herbert went all the direct routes except one and jumped a superb clear round which helped

the team to a bronze medal and rewarded him with an individual silver. Herbert has been German Champion in 1973 and 1975, European Champion with the team and individual silver medallist in 1973. At the 1976 Montreal Olympics and the World Championships in 1978 and 1982 he was part of the silver-medal-winning team. With Feine Dame he went on to win team bronze at the first World Equestrian Games in Stockholm.

'In the ten-minute box the official vet and our team vet had both told me that Feine Dame looked very fit and because she really had given me a very good feeling on the steeplechase and on the roads and tracks, I felt reassured to have a go. Going second to last also gave me the advantage of finding out that, as a whole, the course had jumped well so, although I am usually a cautious rider who likes reaching the finishing post, I felt that I could try it. I really had a dream ride round; Feine Dame gave me such a good feeling over the fences. I was always on time at the minute markers and could even pick up on the time over the last galloping stretch towards the end of the course. Feine Dame really is a "fine lady" on her looks and presence alone! She doesn't like to subordinate herself and wants to be given her own free will. She has always tried to have her own way and I had to adjust to it accordingly. I learnt to let her have more initiative without losing all control. I really had to ride her with feeling and truly treat her like a "fine lady"!'

At the 1994 World Equestrian Games, Australian rider Prue Cribb and Navarone arrived at the second water complex on the cross country at the hottest time of the day. They completed a clear round only a fraction under the optimum time, moving up from tenth place after the dressage to become the overnight leaders. An unlucky three fences down in the show jumping denied Prue the opportunity to become world champion in her first major international competition in the northern hemisphere and she had to settle for ninth place. Although Prue considers this cross country round as their best achievement, the pair have also won Melbourne three day event two years running as well as winning Lochinver in 1992. They also became national champions in 1993.

'As I was approaching the water, team instructions were going through my mind and I just rode as hard as I could down to it. I didn't have a wonderful stride coming into the bounce but Navarone jumped it so boldly, landed in the water and didn't miss a beat. His performance around the whole course was just amazing! He actually isn't a tremendously courageous horse; he soon gets fairly insecure and relies on his confidence. He is not the sort of horse that would grab the bit and get on with his job once he has lost his confidence. I have to be very careful to keep his confidence level up, because once he is confident he will try his hardest. I am the only person that has ever ridden him and we really have a unique relationship. Navarone is very responsive, I just have to change something when I'm riding him and I will feel a change in him immediately. The show jumping result was a big disappointment because in all seven events I rode him in in preparation for the World Championship, he didn't have a rail down. He felt pretty tired on the day and I'm sure that the previous day really took its toll. Navarone has a funny character, he comes across as if he is quite bold and strong-willed but that's only a front as he's actually a bit of a wimp underneath it all. He's not exactly "Einstein" but I shall always remember him as someone very special'

Canadian Young Rider Champion of 1988, Robert Stevenson was second at Fairhill in 1991 on Risky Business which put them in the running for Olympic consideration. The pair travelled to England for the final selection of the 1992 Barcelona Olympics not knowing whether they would make the team as Risky Business had lost some critical time in May and June due to a splint. Luckily the horse recovered well and finished fourth at Savernake, the final Olympic trial for many nations, allowing Robert to fulfil his dream of riding at his first Olympic Games. Because Risky Business was not as fit as he should have been for an event of that calibre, Robert took his partner round a few long routes and managed a clear round, giving his team members valuable support. In the show jumping the horse clearly felt his lack of fitness and had four rails down towards the end of the course. Nowadays, Robert has put competing on the backburner, at least until he has been 'through medical school and out the other side'.

'I chose the long way at the first water, which went round the houses a bit. Risky Business actually hooked a leg jumping into the dark and that was about as close as I came to falling off! So going through the water I certainly felt a huge sense of relief to have that complex out of the way! We were having fun and I was doing what I could to guide him round to save his energy. Risky Business certainly gave me his all in each and every effort. He is an unbelievable character and everywhere he goes he gets new nicknames because he gets along so well with people, preferring to hang around humans than horses! Although his competition name is Risky Business, life with "Will" is anything but risky! He is absolutely one hundred per cent straightforward and anytime he might be short on natural ability, he will make it up with sheer grit and determination. He is completely genuine, lives from the heart and inspires others to do the same'

Riding instructor Sue Hill rode her Irish partner Willowbrook Lad twice round Badminton. The first time was in 1991 when they finished in twenty-ninth place after a run out at the bottom of the Beaufort Staircase. The following year they jumped a double clear and came sixteenth. Jumping into water doesn't seem to startle Sue or Willowbrook Lad, in fact they were the first of only two partnerships who jumped the direct route at the Trout Hatchery during the 1991 Burghley Horse Trials. Sue considers the Burghley clear round, together with her 1992 Badminton placing, as their greatest achievements. Willowbrook Lad has since been retired from eventing because of an injury to his hock and now enjoys life in the field.

'Coming into the fence I knew that if my approach was right at the Badminton Lake and I met it in a balanced way on a good stride, Willowbrook Lad would jump it without any problem. I did, however, worry a bit about turning him once we were in because he was difficult to turn to the left. Riding through the water was probably the worst moment on the

course but Laddy loved his cross country, it was definitely his favourite phase. He was always terribly relaxed and on all the photos I have of him jumping he's got such a calm expression on his face. His ears are always pricked forward and he looks as if he is just looking over his stable door! He is a really lovely person and everyone who meets him falls completely in love with him. I was very lucky to find him because, although he was for sale, his owner couldn't bear to put an advertisement in the paper. It's only because I happened to see them compete at a show that I told the owner I would be interested in buying him if I could sell my horse. She decided immediately that I should have him and generously told me I could pay her once I had the money! At first, his jumping style left a lot to be desired and he used to nearly jump me off over every fence. He improved after months of training and we won the Novice Championship in our first season. Laddy was a real lion across country but I will also say that he was the most non-submissive horse I have ever known!'

Swedish rider Eric Duvander and the Thoroughbred Right On Time had the added pressure of having to produce a clean cross country round in front of their selectors at the 1994 Althorp Championship in the hope of securing a place on the team for the World Equestrian Games. The pair passed the test with flying colours, jumping all the direct routes. Minutes after this picture was taken, Eric was on his way to the airport to catch a plane to Sweden to compete at another event, which meant that they didn't have time to ride their show jumping round. In The Hague the partnership finished in fifteenth place and the year before they were members of the gold-medal-winning team at the European Championship in Achselschwang.

'I was slightly concerned before the start because the top league was competing and a lot of them were crashing but I trusted Right On Time, he gave me a fantastic ride. After having ridden a track like that I always run through it again in my mind. I think about what has happened which I believe is very important because it's only by analysing your rounds that you will improve. I reflect on what I have done and on the feeling the horse has given me. At this particular moment I was asking myself whether Right On Time was truly ready for the World Equestrian Games and I was thinking how convincingly he had just proved himself. But it was a bit of a crazy day and I must admit that I was also concerned about having to rush off immediately to catch my plane! Although Right On Time looked and rode like a pony, he had tremendous scope and felt at home competing with the big boys. He had an incredible heart. I was schooling him in the indoor school – an old converted cow barn – one day and because he used to rush off a bit after his fences, I usually used a wall to slow him down instead of having to pull him in the mouth. The indoor arena had a big, heavy, iron door 1.8 metres high and after we'd had a jump I tried to slow him down against it and Right On Time shortened himself as he normally did in front of a fence but kept going and jumped the door! We landed on concrete but he was perfectly all right, only I was a bit shocked! I didn't know what to do so I went back into the indoor school and continued jumping him! Luckily the people who owned the place realised what had happened and came with a large whisky which was just what I needed!'

Karen Dixon and Too Smart
exit the Second Trout
Hatchery at the 1995
Burghley Horse Trials with
characteristic determination.
They completed in fifth place
at their second attempt

Nigel Taylor and the 12 year old Nick of Time were the last combination on the course at the 1995 Burghley Horse Trials. By the time they reached the Second Trout Hatchery they had incurred two 'uncharacteristic refusals'. Because the ground had been a bit on the firm side, Nigel didn't bother to make up for lost time and remembers that Nick of Time finished the course 'full of running'. Added time penalties, as well as one fence down show jumping, put them into twenty-fifth place at the end of the competition. Earlier in the season Nigel recalls having had a 'lovely ride on him round Badminton' which earned them a place on the short list for the European Championships. Nigel also won his first Armada Dish for having been round Badminton eight times, which inspired him to want a second dish! In 1991 the pair won Blair Castle three day event. The breeders of Nick of Time, Mr and Mrs John Iona-Smith had the horse with Nigel for five years before selling him to former Junior European Team gold medallist, Stephanie Thompson.

'I was sad to see Nick of Time go but at the end of the day, the breeders have to sell a certain amount of horses to finance their operation. Nick of Time is a very brave horse. He's sweet and attentive but knew how to test me in the dressage! He was always excitable but a very careful show jumper. His cross country got better from year to year and I would always start off knowing that I was going to finish. He is the sort of horse that would always have a go at whatever you point him at'

Mark Todd

'If you don't feel slightly sick and nervous at the thought of going round a four-star three day event, there is probably something wrong with you. Not because you are frightened that something terrible is going to happen but it's more the fear of not wanting to make a mistake.'

New Zealander Mark Todd is one of the most remarkable riders the sport of three day eventing has ever seen. Born on 1 March 1956 in Cambridge, New Zealand, at the age of seven he started to ride on a borrowed pony around his grandfather's farm. It wasn't until he was ten that he joined the Pony Club. At sixteen, once he had passed his driving test, Mark started going to shows, mostly show jumping because 'there wasn't much of anything in New Zealand in those days so people did a bit of everything'.

He achieved his first appraisal on Top Hunter a horse Mark did not only get to grade A but which he also qualified for the three day event World Championships in Kentucky in 1978. That same year, Swiss dealer Jürg Zindel, who lived in England at the time, bought Top Hunter and asked Mark to come and work for him in 1979. Mark stayed three years before going back to his native country at the end of 1982, only to return to England two years later. Mark has set up camp in England ever since and lives in Gloucestershire with his New Zealand wife Carolyn and their two children Lauren and James.

Although Mark is mostly a self-taught rider, he remembers fondly his dressage trainers from Pony Club days, Ted Harrison and Locky Richards. Since he came to England, Bill Noble and Hans Eric Pederson have helped him with his dressage. While riding Charisma, he went to Ted Edgar's yard for some show jumping tips. However, Mark believes that watching people has taught him most and that 'Lucinda Green was a very big influence'. Not that he tried to copy her style 'because her style is very flamboyant' and his is 'probably a little more classical' but he admired her 'getting in there and having a go' approach to cross country riding. Through his show jumping experience, Mark is a fairly technical rider. Other riders who watch him carefully have found copying his riding techniques rather difficult, but Mark finds that hard to imagine because he considers himself as a 'thinking rider who allows a horse to get on and do as much his own way as he wants'. Still, there is no doubt that Mark's intuition cannot be copied and that making the most complex fences look as easy as he does must be an art. Despite the fact that his riding looks easy, Mark reckons that: 'It never feels as easy as it looks!' He is convinced that: 'If a horse has been trained to

compete at a high level, it should know what it is doing', and that: 'If one has to beat horses around the course, they shouldn't be there.' Most of the horses he rides have gone through his high level training and he 'lets them get on to do their job as much as possible without interfering'. He will, however, 'help to balance them, hopefully bring them to the fence at the right speed and put them at the right spot to jump, but the rest is up to them and if they need a slap they will get one.' Because he is tall and relatively heavy, he has based his

'Standing at seventeen hands, he's a much bigger horse than I normally like to ride. He is a great jumper and a real athlete.' After coming third at Gatcombe, Mark took his new ride, Bertie Blunt, to Burghley in 1994. Unfortunately, Mark had to deal with the frustration of being eliminated for leaving out a checkpoint on phase C, the second roads and tracks. The judge's decision was made some four hours after the incident had occurred, by which time Mark and Bertie Blunt had completed an immaculate cross country round.

'My side of the coin is that I am not even sure whether I left out the checkpoint; I had to take the judge's word for it. Leaving out the checkpoint meant that I missed 500 metres at a trot speed, which is nothing compared to the entire course. It didn't really give me an advantage. What upset me most was that I wasn't told immediately; they let me go on the cross country course. It's one of the biggest courses in the world, and I think that because I completed before the incident was reported, the judges should have concluded that I didn't gain any advantage and should have left me in the competition'

The British Open Championship at Gatcombe in 1994
was the very first
competition at which Mark
Todd rode Bertie Blunt,
formerly the mount of Nick
Burton. The pair hit it off
immediately and were
placed third behind Karen
Dixon and William Fox-Pitt.

'Gatcombe is not an easy
course. It's not as big as
Badminton or Burghley but
because it runs up- and
downhill with many twists
and turns, it's a real rider's
course. To actually go fast
round Gatcombe, you have
got to take more risks and
ride faster than you would
round other big courses.
This means that you are
actually jumping the fences
at a higher speed, which can
be dangerous. When we got
Bertie Blunt, he was
probably going through a
confidence crisis because he
had fallen at the European
Championships the year
before and was pulled up at
Badminton after having a
fright there. I was
wondering whether I should
be taking him round
Gatcombe. Nick encouraged
me by saying that once I'd
given him a slap, he would
be fine and, in fact, he
was wonderful!'

Riding Just An Ace, Mark Todd acknowledges his fans during the parade which takes place before the final show jumping phase at the 1994 Badminton Horse Trials

theory on 'staying as still as possible when I am in the saddle'. He is aware that 'the more movement there is in the saddle the more tiring it is going to be for the horse'.

Some of Mark's greatest assets must be his sensibility and instinct which he usually demonstrates by reacting in the right way at almost any given moment. He shows compassion when a horse tires and encouragement when his mounts are in need of a quick reminder. He puts this skill down to the sheer volume of horses that have passed through his hands. Riding a lot of horses has helped him to gain insight into his horses' needs, ability and capabilities. He modestly admits to having a 'fairly good sense of timing' which he compares to having a 'built-in clock' which, on the steeplechase and cross country, allows him to 'pretty much know whether you are on time or not'. Knowing how much you can ask from a horse is another skill Mark has acquired over the years. 'When you are riding a lot of horses, you can certainly feel when you can't go any faster; likewise you can feel when a horse is starting to get tired.

Equally, when horses keep on responding when you ask that little bit more, you know they still have a little bit in them.'

However, not all Mark does is as perfectly planned as it seems. Getting to know the course and the individual fences and their alternative routes usually means that Mark will walk round the track two to four times depending on whether he has ridden before at the competition. But he also confessed, with a big grin on his face, that he has set out on the course not knowing where he was going to jump certain fences. He recalls even having changed his mind in 'mid-water at Badminton'.

Mark loves the challenge three day eventing presents. The big build up of tension and the rush of adrenalin, together with the feeling of being on a high when things have gone well, are emotions he simply would not want to miss. He even goes as far as admitting that although he gets 'a great buzz out of riding in a show jumping Grand Prix', nothing else compares to 'riding across country on a good horse'.

One of Mark's greatest disappointments during the 1994 season was his fall at the water during the World Equestrian Games in The Hague. At the point where this picture was taken, Mark recalls that Just An Ace 'felt fabulous, making fences look so easy', and that what happened was 'just such rotten luck'. The pair were on a better dressage score than the eventual World Champion, Vaughn Jefferis, on Bounce, and Mark still feels that Just an Ace 'should have won the title'. 'He felt really great and he is such a good jumper. He's probably the best horse I have ever ridden that never wins a big competition. I hope that I am proven wrong and he goes on to win Badminton!'

When talking about the importance of dressage within the context of the entire competition, Mark believes that, although it is not his favourite phase, 'it is very important in terms of the whole competition' because, 'if you don't have a good dressage, you haven't got much chance of being in the first three'. Mark also admits to finding the dressage phase not testing enough and would like 'to see the test made more difficult'. He enhances his criticism by commenting on the way horses are judged and claims that 'the test is relying too much on how well a horse moves instead of putting more emphasis on the horse's training'. He would like to see movements such as canter half-pass added so that sitting on 'a flashy mover that stays calm' would not be the judges' only criterion.

One of Mark's greatest disappointments during the 1994 season was his fall at the water during the World Equestrian Games in The Hague. Mark recalls that Just An Ace 'felt fabulous and that he was going so easily'. He puts what happened in The Hague down to 'rotten luck'. Mark still doesn't know what actually caused the pair to fall. 'There might have been a dip in the ground, or he might have stood on

Following Mark Todd through my 300 mm lens as he cruised through the water complex at Badminton 1993 was a real pleasure. I could hardly believe the enthusiasm with which Just An Ace responded to Mark's aids. Witnessing the horse's athleticism, grace and the complete trust and harmony the two exuded brought a big smile to my face. I couldn't wait to ask Mark whether it felt as easy to them as it had looked.

'The water complex at Badminton is certainly a milestone on the course and if you are clear up to there, you are starting to feel more confident. On Just An Ace, a horse with such a good jumping technique, my job is made much easier. He's a very bold water jumper. He's very neat, quick thinking as well as very athletic. When

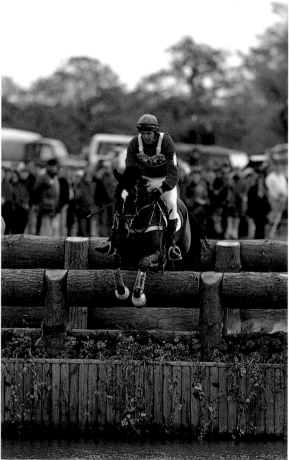

his overreach boot. I only remember that I felt him almost getting ready to jump when, instead of doing just that, he went head first into the bank. He hit it so hard that he actually broke his nose.' The blow of the fall was just as hard for Mark. All he could think of was that his 'chances had just gone within a split second'. Just An Ace seemed OK and Mark really didn't feel like walking home, so he decided 'to canter round the rest of the course'. His decision to carry on not only showed Mark's enormous strength of character, it also turned out to be of vital importance for the team. Mark admits to not being

aware of that at the time, but finishing meant that New Zealand ended the competition in sixth place which qualified them for the Olympics in Atlanta.

It is thanks to Mark's tremendous achievements that three day eventing has become one of New Zealand's 'higher profile sports'. His most notable successes include two consecutive Olympic gold medals on Charisma in 1984 in Los Angeles and 1988 in Seoul; two wins at Badminton in 1980 on Southern Comfort and 1994 on Horton Point; and first and second at Burghley in 1987 with Wilton Fair and Charisma, as well as two other Burghley wins in 1990

we were coming to the water, there was never the question in my mind whether he was going to stop. My job was to present him at the right position for the first obstacle. He helped me get there because he was so keen to jump it and yet he was listening to me. We came to the bounce and there is actually very little one can do in a bounce situation except to keep one's leg on and make sure the horse keeps going forward. Just An Ace landed very safely in the water, so I could already look to the next jump without having to worry about his landing. He kept travelling through the water very well, which meant that I didn't have to kick him on. I was just sitting there, balancing . . .

with Face The Music and in 1991 on Welton Greylag. Mark has also clinched first places in other prestigious events such as Luhmühlen, Germany 1986 and Saumur, France 1987, both on the formidable Charisma, and Stockholm, Sweden 1989 on Welton Greylag, just one year before acquiring a team gold medal at the World Equestrian Games with Balhua. Mark has certainly been a pioneer for the sport and his indisputable horsemanship, together with his accomplishments, have been so influential that it came as no surprise when team-mates Blyth Tait and Vaughn Jefferis breathed down Mark's neck

at Badminton 1994 and the Kiwis took the first three places.

He first hit the headlines as a 24 year old when winning Badminton in 1980 at his first attempt. Mark remembers that it was 'actually pretty remarkable' because as a child he had read books about Badminton, thinking that it was 'something unattainable, a dream really'.

Winning Badminton some fourteen years later in 1994, on Horton Point, a horse Mark had only known for five days, was 'the oddest feeling'. His colleagues, the media and fans alike would call that achievement

. . . him and he just popped out the other end. The joy about riding Just An Ace across country is that he loves doing it so much. He is so confident in his ability and it is almost a case of sitting there and steering. The difficulty at this particular water combination was that the bounce was only twelve feet wide, which is very short for a bounce, but because of the water it makes horses back off so one really has to ride it a lot stronger than one normally would for a twelve-feet bounce. It is also very important to keep one's line and maintain the rhythm. I remember having had a wonderful feeling on him there. It was almost as if we were through it before it had even happened'

just as remarkable because the first time he rode the chestnut gelding was the day before the start of the competition. That was only for twenty minutes as 'he went perfectly well on the flat and we seemed to get on', which prompted Mark to conclude that 'there was no point in doing any more'. In fact, Horton Point felt so good that Mark told the Bevan sisters, 'That'll do, put him away.'

His relaxed and easy going nature, together with his impressive record of achievements, lends guidance to a philosophical outlook on life. Nowadays, Mark does not set his goals as high as he used to. In 1994 he wanted to win Badminton again and become world champion in The Hague. He won Badminton but 'the games went down the drain' and at this stage in his life he believes that the chances of becoming world champion again are 'pretty slim'. However, let us not be fooled too much by Mark's nonchalant modesty because, although he has achieved more than 'I ever dreamed I would' and he does not have any 'burning ambition such as winning Gold at the Sydney Olympics', he 'loves winning' and at every competition he goes to he will give it his 'best shot'.

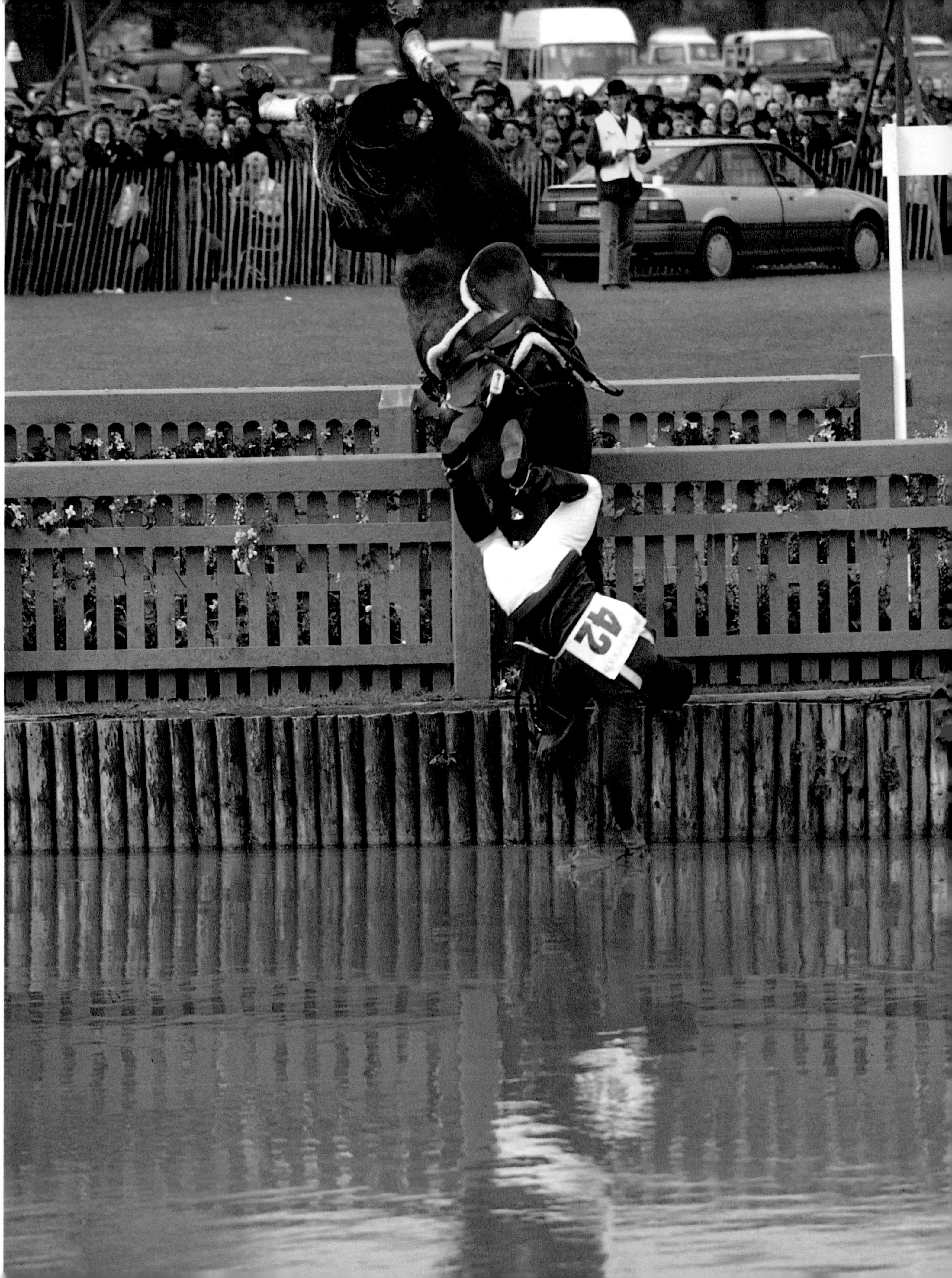
42

MISHAPS

One thing that impressed me most when putting this chapter together was the sporting way in which the riders have reacted to telling me about their misfortunes. Understandably, those riders who are featured only in this chapter felt that it was unfortunate for their horse to be photographed having a mishap because the pictures don't do their horses justice. Most riders are so proud of their horses' ability and courage that they would prefer them to be remembered for a super jump and not for the odd occasion when things had gone wrong. I am grateful to the riders for being so humble and willing to share these moments which has enabled me to show the other side of the sport.

From a photographic point of view, there is no doubt that a fall adds drama to a picture but I still prefer action-packed shots that show the dynamic nature of the sport and capture the rider's concentration as well as the horse's effort. The trust between horse and rider becomes far more apparent when things go right and they jump well. However, there is always a good reason why horses and riders have parted company and I am pleased to say that neither the horses nor their riders shown in this chapter were seriously injured. I was amazed how the riders could recall what happened in such graphic detail, especially as some time has passed since the

fall and incidents such as these happen so quickly. For me it's a further proof of their professionalism and there is no doubt that lessons are learnt from these experiences.

I have evented at Novice level in Austria and I remember having a crashing fall on an English Thoroughbred my parents owned at the time. The horse had put me through a lot of agony earlier on the course when he had run out twice at a small jump into water, determined not to get his feet wet. It took some persistence on my behalf finally to get this fence behind us! Wanting to make up for lost time, I carried on flat out which proved to be a grave mistake because when we came to the penultimate fence, a closed obstacle of two jumps set at one stride, my enthusiasm in wanting to reach the finish proved to be too much. We had a crashing fall coming into the obstacle and it is only because my father was standing there that I found out afterwards what had actually gone wrong. High Leap tried to bounce the two jumps and couldn't quite make it! Luckily we both got up none the worse for it, cleared the fence at the second attempt and, believe it or not, finished the course within the optimum time! Next day he jumped a smooth and faultless show jumping round but my inexperience had certainly shone through and it is really only since I have seen

Gloucestershire-based New Zealander Andrew Bennie and Lismore had already had two stops on the course before they came to grief at the Badminton lake in 1991. Although the mare had qualified, Andrew thinks with hindsight that because of her health problems, she wasn't really up to it.

'Lismore had had some problems with her heart earlier in the season and therefore she didn't have a good lead up to the event. On the cross country day she was backing off all along. As we got to the lake, she jumped the first part of the bounce and tried to stop at the second but, because she is a big heavy mare, she chested it, did a forward roll over her shoulder and into the water. Luckily neither of us got hurt, just my pride! Lismore was a very good and competitive horse, very honest, and, at the end of the day, had she been one hundred per cent fit, I'm sure that she would have made it round. I would describe her as a big bossy woman!'

the top eventers at work that I realised how much there is to the sport. Talking to the riders also made me realise how important it is not to let one's concentration wane especially when something does go wrong because it is mostly in those situations that riders and horses learn and hopefully improve.

The pictures in the following pages certainly highlight the degree of danger that inevitably goes hand in hand with the sport. The mishaps emphasise the level of risk that riders take once they start on the cross country phase. Their bravery and desire to perform well can only be admired.

Dutch rider Eddy Stibbe started his eventing career in Holland, alongside his commitments in the family business. He has competed in over 150 three day events and was placed in more than 75. At the 1991 Badminton Horse Trials, however, he sadly parted company with Kilmacthomas at the lake. Previously, the pair had won Saumur in 1990.

'Kilmacthomas backed off the fence a little bit so I had to put my leg on and he landed just too close to the bounce, couldn't stop himself and over we went! Because of his height and power, he would often overjump combinations and, as he wasn't the brainiest of horses, it could end in a fall. In the air over the first fence I knew that he was going to land too deep to the next fence and that we were going to fall. All that happened was that we got wet! I have been eventing so long now and through all the ups and downs of the sport, that picking myself up after a fall is not too difficult anymore. You just have to take the falls as they come!'

German rider Andreas Weiser and his Irish horse Poker Face competed at the 1994 World Equestrian Games as individuals. Before they came to the second water complex, the pair had already suffered a run out for which Andreas blames rider error. As they approached the water fence, Poker Face decided to run out again and deposited Andreas on the log, sparing him the discomfort of getting wet. The horse was easy enough to catch and, after jumping the alternative at the water, the pair finished the course and the competition with a clear show jumping round.

'Actually I had quite a good feeling before I started on phase D, although I knew that the heat factor would play a considerable role. I can't really understand why we had difficulties at that fence. He might have jumped in too big and didn't have enough room to bounce out. But falling off happens so quickly that it is difficult to think about it. The only thing to do at the time is to get back on, continue and finish the course, that is the main thing. Poker Face is normally a real trier and a fighter across country but I believe that this mishap was probably a result of our previous run out. If a horse has had one run out, a second one can easily follow and I am sure that the trust between horse and rider had suffered slightly. Poker Face is a bit of an individualist who wants to be left alone but he can also blow up quite easily, especially in the dressage. He is a fantastic horse that will give his very best even when he might feel slight muscle fatigue. He is halfway between genius and sheer madness. My wife named him Poker Face because he can be a little cunning at times'

Rodney Powell had a premonition about falling in the lake before he came to Badminton in 1994. The Dealer and Rodney survived the lake but were caught out only a few fences later by the Vicarage Pond. Despite having a thorough drenching, they managed to complete the course. However, The Dealer has now retired from three day eventing and is pursuing a less hazardous career in show jumping.

'I think that the horse didn't come up high enough with his front legs. He got caught up on the front of the fence and I buckled on landing. The water in there is filthy! Nobody likes falling; your pride and confidence get knocked more than anything else, but it's not so bad if you have a good horse to get back on. They can help you to regain your self-esteem. I'm sure that the same applies to horses. It's good of them to carry on after a fall and it's up to the rider to restore confidence in his horse. The Dealer had a mind of his own; he was the most arrogant horse you'd ever wish to meet. We got along really well!'

Before coming to Burghley in 1994, Daisy Dick and Little Victor had already won Windsor in 1992, followed by a team gold medal at the European Young Riders Championship in 1993. Unfortunately, they suffered a crashing fall towards the end of the course at their first attempt. 'Little Victor had actually been going brilliantly up till then. As he came down to the Hanging Log, he was looking underneath the fence. I thought I had approached it well but he just dropped a leg, panicked and down we went. As soon as his leg touched down, I knew that we

were going to turn over. I just remember hitting the ground, looking up and seeing his large body coming down on top of me. He winded me quite badly and I sat on the ground for a while, but he soon stood up. He was winded too so I decided to call it a day. The fall was really devastating because he had given me such a great ride. We were only four fences from home and I still wish now that somebody could tell me what went wrong! He was fine the next day and would have trotted up sound. I absolutely adore Little Victor. We could be offered anything for him and he wouldn't leave the yard. They could take all the others but not him. He is like my brother'

Tanya Cleverly didn't quite manage to stay on the right side of Watkins while tackling the lake at Badminton in 1994. Their stunt certainly kept the crowds entertained and many of them would probably not have remembered that the same pair had completed Badminton in third place only the year before. Watkins and Tanya also share a good track record at Burghley by being placed five times.

'As I came to make my line to the fence, I wasn't really paying attention and Watkins and I got stuck behind a dip and I missed my stride. He hit the first part of the bounce combination shoulder-high which, at the speed you would be travelling to get into the lake, catapulted me out of the saddle. I came off to the right but he got his legs out, carried on beautifully and bounced himself into the lake with ears pricked and I landed on my backside! The first emotion or thought that went through my mind was: "Oh my God, that's it, I have blown it!". I was really cross with myself, not with Watkins because I knew that I had put him slightly wrong. Then I just laughed because the crowd is so huge round the lake and they were delighted with my spectacular fall! Watkins stupidly wandered off down the lake and wouldn't come back. I wasn't going to make more of a fool of myself by wallowing in the deep water. A spectator very gallantly took off his jacket, dived in and brought Watkins, all tangled in the TV cables, back to me. I was so grateful to him. Watkins is very sensible and laid back. I am sure he must have felt the pull on his legs and that's why he didn't come back. He has world class ability but I have a bit of a struggle keeping him together because he is so long. I always thought that I should perhaps sell him to a man but the amount of pleasure Watkins has given me is just unbeatable. He is a gentle giant and I love him to death. I went through a bit of a rough time when my marriage broke up and he was the only thing that kept me going. Watkins just picked up the feelings I was having and I'm sure that if he could have spoken, he would have said: "Never mind, come on, dust yourself off and start all over again." '

Former school teacher Gill Rolton from Adelaide, South Australia admitted that she didn't have one of her best weekends competing at the 1994 World Equestrian Games in The Hague on Peppermint Grove. One refusal at each of the two water fences and one fence down in the show jumping meant that they finished the competition in forty-first place. This was not up to the pair's usual standard for they had earned their place on the team with some outstanding performances. The then ten-year-old Peppermint Grove and Gillian had been members of the gold-medal-winning team at the Barcelona Olympics. Since The Hague, they have become the 1995 Australian Champions, completing the competition on their dressage score of 48.

'At the World Equestrian Games Peppermint Grove wasn't a well horse; he actually had quite a temperature before he even started the cross country. He had an allergy to the shavings and wasn't himself, he didn't take me into the fences the way he usually would. I don't normally ever hit him going into water but he was backing off the fence a little so I gave him a tap behind my leg and because he didn't jump in big enough he didn't make the distance through the water to the wall. There wasn't enough room for three strides and we didn't have enough impulsion for two. I probably got a bit in front of the movement instead of sitting up and keeping him in balance so he got in deep and tried to scramble over but I pulled him off and jumped the option. He didn't hurt himself but it did upset his confidence which is why we had another stop at the second water. Peppermint Grove is quite arrogant but the most wonderful and courageous friend. He is a fantastic athlete and very forgiving. Even when I'm wrong he usually gets me out of trouble'

Stewart Christie made a name for himself in the sport bringing many young horses up through the ranks to Advanced level. In 1988 he took The Magistrate to his third Badminton where the pair had a most unfortunate and uncharacteristic ride from the start. Before reaching the infamous Normandy Bank, they had encountered problems at previous obstacles, including a stop at fence four where The Magistrate ran into the corner of the fence, injuring his shoulder and losing his rider for the first time, as well as a refusal and fall at fence six. The Magistrate did, however, have an impeccable record from 1982, completing Burghley and Badminton twice, and scoring a marvellous double clear round at Badminton in 1986.

'The Magistrate had clearly been in a bit of pain jumping round the course. You had to bounce the Normandy Bank and couldn't afford to take a stride on top but he took a little shuffle and everything seemed to happen in slow motion. I remember the horse taking off and touching down again, almost going over. His shoulders got to the fence and the forward momentum nearly carried him but then I continued and he didn't! I was a bit shaken and the horse too, so we called it a day. Luckily the experience didn't damage him mentally but he did have a stressed shoulder. I didn't hurt myself in the least funnily enough after a fall as spectacular as this. People tend to think that the rider must be absolutely wrecked but I was actually fine! The only disappointment is that you are trying to maintain your form and, in particular, keep the horse's record as clean as possible. A situation like this is sad because the horse doesn't deserve to go out like this. It's like boxers; once they get flattened for the last time it's a pity because they have been on top of the world before that! The only way I remember The Magistrate is for being one of the bravest horses I have ridden'

French breeder and event rider Pascal Leroy frightened a lot of people, including himself, when he and Logical Song came to grief jumping into the lake at the 1991 Badminton Horse Trials. The fall could have turned nasty if Pascal had not succeeded in releasing his foot from the stirrup in time. Luckily he did and Logical Song wandered off into the middle of the lake. A delighted crowd watched as the photographer known as Gipsy Joe plunged into cold water to retrieve the horse. The Frenchman took it all in his stride, remounted Logical Song and completed the course without any further incidents. The pair put on a brave face on the final day and finished the competition in forty-fifth place. At that time the duo were one of the best in France and qualified for the 1991 European Championships. Nevertheless, Pascal accepted a good offer for the horse from Japan shortly before the championships.

'That year two uprights that weren't exactly parallel to one another led into the lake and I had chosen to tackle the fence in the middle. As we got closer, Logical Song was looking at the crowds and when I pushed him to bounce out he decided to touch down again, trying to put in an extra stride before jumping into the lake. He caught the second fence with his knees and over we went. I was worried for a moment because if my foot had stayed in the stirrup I would have landed underneath the horse. But it all worked out and I only had a bruised hand when Logical Song stood on it with his studs. But I never thought of not getting back on. After all, the name of the game is to reach the finishing post. In hindsight, I think that I should have kept more to one side when jumping the fence because the distance was longer and, knowing my horse, I'm sure that he would have had the space

to put in the little shuffle he needed. Logical Song was a very cool, level-headed horse, especially in difficult situations. He hadn't stopped once during our partnership but he lacked that extra bit of pep and we had our problems when distances were a bit long. He was a cold, emotionless horse and most definitely lacked a bit of magic. He always completed the cross country courses but he wasn't the fastest and at one stage I nicknamed him "Diesel"! Still, Logical Song has been my faithful and courageous companion for eight years I do owe him a lot, most of all the privilege of having been round Badminton. I have excellent memories of it and I would love to try it again. One does, after all, earn worldwide respect if one has a good ride round the course. Technically, the course is hell!'

Julian Trevor-Roper hit the headlines when he won the
inaugural Eventers Special class at Hickstead in 1990. A year
later, this time on Nigel Taylor's Morning Town II, Julian
thought he had a good chance of winning it again. A stop at
the small white rail at the top of the Hickstead Bank meant
that the pair didn't go forward to the jump off and had to
content themselves with sixth place. They went on to show
jump successfully that season, winning £600 and only
narrowly missing out on qualifying for the Foxhunter final
at Wembley. They also finished nineteenth at Blenheim
that year.

'Before I went into the arena, Nigel told me that there
was only one place on the course to be thoughtful about,
and that's where he stopped! I adored riding Morning Town,
he was such a careful jumper. As an event horse he was just
bordering on being slightly too cautious. Morning Town
needed confidence from the rider all the way through
everything he did. I knew that he wouldn't have a fence
down and, trotting up the bank just being asked to help
himself, he didn't have the confidence to do it. But whatever
you jumped with him, whether it was a crossed pole or a big
fence, he was the same, he absolutely loved it. The main
arena at Hickstead is amazing. A lot of horses go in and are
overawed by the atmosphere and many experienced horses
can jump very green there. Event horses are funny really,
they go out and jump all these big fences across country and
then they go in the ring and spook at a little water tray
because they are not used to jumping it. However good the
horse, you can never tell what it is going to do at Hickstead'

THE
SHOW JUMPING

With the imposing challenges of the cross country and the scrutiny of the final veterinary inspection behind them, competitors embark on the show jumping, the last leg of the three day event.

On the morning of the final day and before riders tackle the show jumping, they have to present their horses to the ground jury to see whether they are fit to complete the competition. This all important aspect of the three day event cannot be underestimated because the horses' welfare comes first and the ground jury will not hesitate to fail a competitor if there is a question mark concerning a horse's soundness. At major events such as Badminton the veterinary inspection attracts a very large crowd eager to watch the proceedings carefully. Part of their fun is not only to judge for themselves whether a horse is sound or not, but also to see the riders smartly dressed up for the occasion. The veterinary inspection can play a significant role and influence the classification at this stage of the competition if leading contenders are not allowed to

continue. A recent example of this was at Badminton in 1995 when William Fox-Pitt and Chaka were leading after the speed and endurance phase, only to fail the veterinary inspection. William's hopes of winning this prestigious event were shattered there and then. Ian Stark will remember the Barcelona Olympics with the same kind of disappointment because Murphy Himself was 'spun' at the final inspection and not allowed to continue in the competition. If riders have the slightest doubts about the soundness of their horse, they usually decide to withdraw without presenting it.

With the trot up behind them, competitors approach the final phase with a certain amount of apprehension, especially if their horse is not a careful show jumper and they are among the top contenders. This is not a stage for the faint hearted because the atmosphere in the show jumping arena can be electric, especially when the competition builds to a climax as the last horses go in in reverse order of merit. The riders are often anxious if they are riding a tired horse and will

Ian Stark and Murphy Himself, Barcelona Olympics – a dejected Ian Stark being consoled after Murphy was 'spun' at the final veterinary inspection

Karen Dixon with Get Smart. A very smart turn-out for the veterinary inspection at the 1992 Barcelona Olympics!

(Right) Bruce Davidson and Mystic High, Badminton, 1991 – Bruce appears to be on a high during the final veterinary inspection!

endeavour to save it as much as possible from any unnecessary stress. A lot will depend on a good warm up period. Riders will hope that any stiffness their horse might feel will disappear with careful preparation. Again, it's very much a case of knowing your horse and how he is feeling. At this stage, riders are often helped by their show jumping trainers who offer them their expertise and support. The pressure on riders is evident before they jump and they are quick to show their relief when they have jumped a good round. Compared to pure show jumping, penalties in the show jumping phase of three day eventing are marked more severely, with one fence down costing five penalties and the first refusal ten, followed by twenty for the second. The slightest

The Ground Jury confer at
the second veterinary
inspection of the 1992
Barcelona Olympics

mistake can therefore mean the difference between winning and losing. Usually the top contenders lie very closely together, often only separated by one fence or less which means that the winner is not decided until the last horse has jumped. The fences are not as high as they are for pure show jumping because it is not so much the jumping ability that is tested but more a test to show that the horses are supple and have recovered from the demands of the previous day. For the rider this phase is, above all, a true test of nerves!

When photographing the show jumping phase, I am always keen to catch horses travelling through a combination because riders usually sit up and look straight ahead to the next fence. This will increase my chances of producing a shot that shows horse and rider in balance and hopefully jumping in a good style. What is also nice is to capture them between fences when a concentrated expression, full of anticipation, can illustrate the tension they feel in that moment. I also prefer to photograph horses over a spread as opposed to a vertical because even a tired horse will most probably put more effort into jumping an oxer than a flimsy-looking stile, for example. Horses are airborne that little bit longer and, because they have more time to square up their front legs, it will result in a worthier picture.

To give readers a better understanding of the technical aspects of designing a show jumping course for three day events, I have asked Alan Oliver to share his ideology in the following pages.

jumper, both competing and designing courses, has given him the necessary skills which he has successfully transferred to the eventing arena. As an FEI official designer, he builds courses for all levels of competition, from Novice to International standard. The Royal Windsor Horse Show and the Horse of the Year Show rank among some of the more prestigious shows in England where he has built. Designing all year round, his job has taken him across the world, including South Africa and Australia. Alan considers building the courses for the 1988 Gothenburg Volvo World Cup Final as one of his most exciting projects. However, his skills are just as much in demand in the world of eventing, where he builds the show jumping courses at both one and three day events. Among the higher profile eventing courses he has built are the British Open Championships at Gatcombe, Cornbury Park and the international three day event at Blenheim.

Born into a farming family near Aylesbury in Buckinghamshire, Alan's love for horses was inherited from his father and grandfather who had always been in the business of buying and selling horses. He first rode at the age of four and a life with horses seemed inevitable. 'I never knew anything else but riding horses and driving a tractor.' Only a few months after Alan rode at Olympia as a Junior in 1939, the Second World War broke out which meant that all horse shows were suspended until 1946. Nevertheless, his father kept a few horses throughout the war years and, as soon as the shows resumed, Alan continued competing. 'It was totally different in those days. The

Alan Oliver

Show jumping courses for eventing present different questions to the tracks of pure show jumping but it is important for the designer to have a thorough knowledge and understanding of both disciplines. Alan Oliver is a man whose vast experience as a show

Llewellyn, Peter Robeson and Pat Smythe. Alan was a member of four victorious British teams in London and Rotterdam, he won the Victor Ludorum at the Horse of the Year Show three years running and became national champion on five occasions. During the winter months he also point-to-pointed and enjoyed hunting.

In the sixties, Alan developed an interest in course designing and started to build while he was still show jumping. Having competed for more than 30 seasons, he was beginning to get a little bored with it and 'was lucky enough to meet up with people who wanted me to build at the shows they ran'. It was soon after that that he fell into 'big league designing' when Major Reg Whitehead was taken ill and asked Alan to help him build at the Devon County and Bath & West shows. 'I found it fascinating and thought that it probably wouldn't be as much hard work as

season began at Easter and finished at the end of September and then in 1949 it ended with the Horse of the Year Show which was first held at Haringey.' His best achievements were between 1951 and 1972 when he rode with some of the greatest names in show jumping, including Wilf White, Harry

riding horses!' But life in the fast lane of course designing, with assignments almost every weekend, has made Alan change his mind.

Although Alan never competed in eventing, he got involved in the sport during his marriage to well-known event trainer Alison Oliver. 'We helped each other and I used to put up the fences when Princess

Bruce Davidson's groom putting the finishing touches to Squelch before their show jumping round at Blenheim in 1994

Anne was training with us.' It was then that Alan realised that the eventers tackled their show jumps in a different way to the show jumpers and ever since he began designing courses for eventing he has cultivated his craft to a fine art.

'Every course I design for the eventers is a real challenge, especially when I build at one day events because my course is jumped before the cross country. I usually have to deal with a tremendous number of horses, some of which may be ridden by less experienced riders and one really has to get a feel for it because I don't want to put them in awkward situations. I like to build a course that flows

and gets most of the horses round. If I can get about fifty per cent clear in the Novice, as well as the Advanced sections, I believe I have done a reasonably good job. Although these horses are supposed to jump the difficult fences on the cross country, I still have to come up with some sort of test but it has to be done in a subtle way. I have to have a few related distances because riders should be made to think a little bit. If I can, I will use a bit of undulating ground and play with running them up and downhill or let them jump on a slight incline. I also have to adjust my courses to the level of the competition. Novice and Pre-novice horses have to be even more encouraged into going forward because I don't want to frighten them by having fences down before they face the most challenging phase. For the Advanced sections I will have a few turns because the aim is to keep horses more balanced but the last thing I want is for horses and riders to lose their confidence.'

When building at a three day event, Alan has to rethink his strategy slightly and he believes that when the show jumping is held on the final day, courses have to be designed a little differently. 'At an event such as Blenheim, you have to test the horses' jumping ability but give them plenty of room because they have been used to galloping across country. I don't want to shorten them too much. Horses shouldn't have to back off their fences because it would be too much against their nature after having gone flat out the day before. It also helps when I know what they have been asked to jump the day before and what the condition of the ground was like. What I am really testing on the final day is whether the horse is fit and supple enough to come out and jump a clean round. In fact it's not the course designer who sorts out the horses; I believe that they have done that themselves before they even get to me. It's more the riders that are tested for their

that they are walking the course, and even more so when they are actually riding their round.'

Alan feels that riders used to take the show jumping phase much too casually, which meant that they inevitably dropped down the order considerably when they didn't get the final phase right. 'I am certain that eventers have changed their attitude

Bruce Davidson enjoying a quick cigarette before collecting first prize for winning Blenheim in 1994

ability to concentrate. The best horse and rider combination nearly always wins. The riders have got to know exactly where they are going. The majority of them just wander around not really registering where the fences are, their angle or related distance and this is where they can be caught out. I believe that riders have to be alert during the entire time

significantly. They are taking the show jumping much more seriously because a couple of fences down can suddenly move them from the top three to well below tenth place. I think that during the first three months of the year about forty per cent of the horses that jump indoors are eventers preparing for the season.'

Lying third after speed and endurance at the 1992 Barcelona Olympics, German rider Herbert Blöcker focused on jumping a clear round in the show jumping phase. Knowing that the then seventeen-year-old mare Feine Dame could easily knock a fence down when going too fast, the pair chose a definitely slower rhythm than across country and collected one and a half time faults on an otherwise superbly judged trip. Their effort was rewarded with the individual silver and team bronze medals. 'German show jumper Franke Sloothaak helped us in the collecting ring and although Feine Dame did feel the efforts of the previous day a little bit, she still had a lot in her and didn't give any signs of tiredness. All the German show jumpers were full of enthusiasm and said that they wanted me and Feine Dame on the team for the Nations Cup! I wasn't really nervous, I just thought about riding my round. I was so pleased that she had jumped well, exceeding the time didn't really matter at that stage, besides I didn't really register that it had won me two medals. It only dawned on me when the entire team came rushing up to congratulate me. It was as if Feine Dame really knew how much it had mattered. Somehow I prefer riding mares. If one can empathise with sensitive mares, they are usually prepared to give you everything'

Whether Alan is designing pure show jumping courses or tracks for the eventers, he knows that being flexible is a vital asset in his job. Only seldom does he know exactly what the terrain and weather conditions are going to be. When building abroad he will sometimes know what material he will encounter only when he arrives at the showground.

'One year at the Royal Windsor Horse Show the ground had been fairly hard so the organisers decided to water the arena. Unfortunately, it turned out to be like a quagmire because not only did the King's Troop and the Household Cavalry perform on it, the driving people also had their obstacle course in the arena. By the time I had to build the Area International Trial, I told my men to forget the plans I had given them in the morning and that we were just going to build the fences on the good patches we could find! I never turn up at a showground with ready-made plans because you don't know whether organisers have decided to changed the dimensions or location of the arena. It can happen that they have suddenly decided to change the water fence and if I had four days of course plans with me in a situation like that, I could just throw them away. I didn't have any plans when I arrived at the Scandinavium in Gothenburg to build the World Cup Final because I didn't know what material was going to be available. Of course, I have a certain idea in my mind but I can really only do my job when I get a feel for the arena and know what I can use. In Gothenburg I also had the added challenge of all the flower arrangements and islands they put in, so I told them to go ahead with their design and that I would simply build my fences around them!'

Inspiration is another key to successful course designing and Alan finds his in the most peculiar situations. 'I might be driving along and see some jumps in a field that look a bit different and I would pull up because I believe that you can learn something from every fool. You can even pick up something from ten or twelve-year-old children who have built a fence in a field with barrels, bits of twigs, straw bales or whatever they find. I am forever asking myself what I could do next because I generally like to come up with something different. I often get to work with the same type of material but, by changing it around a little, you can alter the whole design. I just play around with the material, trying to make it as attractive as possible to the public.'

Over the years, Alan has noticed a real contrast between the people involved in eventing and those that purely show jump. 'The main difference lies in their attitude to the sport in general and in their behaviour towards their horses. Eventers don't grumble or whinge about the courses! If I build a course a little big, the eventers would come and talk to me about it if they are worried. Show jumpers would complain immediately because all they are interested in is whether they can win the big prize money. Eventers see the course more like a challenge, they would even ask advice on how to ride a certain related distance. They are generally much easier to get along with, they come into the arena smiling and not stone-faced and grizzly like the show

jumpers. Another characteristic of the eventers is that they will come up and thank me if they feel the course rode well. It does make a difference when you are appreciated for what you are trying to achieve. The pure show jumpers would just walk away from you, believing that they should compete against the course designer, whereas the eventers know that they can work with you. I also get the feeling that the eventers care more about their horses, perhaps because they spend that much more time with the same horse. They spend many hours schooling their horses for the dressage, then they get their horses fit and train for the jumping. All a show jumper has in mind is to go down to this fence and jump it as clean as he can.'

Alan's views on the format of three day eventing are 'a little old fashioned' in as much as he believes that it should stay the way it is. 'Ending the competition on the show jumping can be very exciting. I have seen Richard Meade lose Badminton on three-quarters of a time fault! I also think that, mentally, three day event horses know that when they have done the show jumping they have finished. But what I do want to see changed is the dimensions of the fences at three- and four-star events. I think that one could easily raise the occasional fence from 1.2 to 1.3 metres and that the width could be stretched to two metres. I am not in favour of a water jump unless it's built with poles over it. I don't build open water jumps because I don't want to confuse the horse that had to jump into water the day before or whenever it goes across country and then ask it to clear the water in a different phase of the competition.'

One of Alan's greatest ambitions is to be asked to build the Olympics or a world championship because it would give him the biggest thrill to see not only the best in the world but the best from every nation tackle his course. 'The challenge I'm looking for is to build for everybody, the top of the sport and at the same time taking the lesser countries into account. You would have to get the less experienced competitors around the course without breaking their necks, hopefully. I want to produce good

competitions that competitors enjoy riding in. I also get a lot of pleasure out of encouraging young horses and up and coming riders. I like to see riders having a go, hoping that they'll want to keep coming back.'

Helen Bell and Troubleshooter have a good track record at Badminton, finishing third in 1991, tenth in 1993 and ninth in 1994, and look as concentrated as ever on their way to a clear show jumping round.

'The pressure of doing the final phase is probably the worst feeling in the world. Show jumping has always been nerve wrecking for me. Troubleshooter is very good at it and if I give him any sort of chance, he'll jump clean but I can very often get it wrong and ruin it for him! He has got a heart as big as a lion which he proved at the World Equestrian Games and at the European Championships by staying clear across country. You can't ask for more really. Troubleshooter is as bold as brass and cheeky with it'

Robert Lemieux and Just An Ace having just completed their round in the newly introduced Eventer's Show Jumping class during the CSIO meeting at Hickstead in 1990, where they finished in second place behind Julian Trevor-Roper and Airborne Max. The pair had only competed in two three day events: Bramham where they came second and Burghley where they finished in fourteenth place before Mark Todd took over the ride.

'Just An Ace is one of the best thinking horses I have ever ridden. He thinks his way around everything he does; he's like a radar. He has the ability to lock on to something and do things almost on auto-pilot'

Tiny Clapham and Brother Jack share the same enthusiasm while testing their scope over the Eventer's Show Jumping track during the 1991 Hickstead CSIO meeting. Most riders like that class because they feel that they should be stretched by a slightly more demanding show jumping test. The only frustrating thing is that it usually clashes with a major three day event.

'That's what I would call the jockey throwing her heart over! Brother Jack is the nicest horse to show jump; he could pretty well guarantee you a clean round. But he can also be cheeky and try you out. He is full of character and will always have a special place in my heart because I bought him as a six year old when he was completely unridable. We had a couple of sessions in the indoor school. I'd be riding him and it would be like riding the wall of death! You'd be giving him a kick sometimes and he'd go straight up and you'd be bouncing off the wall. Eventually he realised that I wasn't going to get off and so he conceded. Jack is a little man with a big heart who sadly lacks a bit of movement but he is a real fun horse'

King Kong and Mary King completed Burghley 1994 in second place with an immaculate show jumping round.

'It was exciting with King Kong because it was his first four-star event and you never quite know how good their jumping will be on the third day after such an extreme effort the day before. While warming him up I felt he had a real spring to his jump which he fortunately maintained when he got in the ring. King Kong jumped as well, if not better than he had at one day events. It's lovely to know that you're on a horse that can jump because there is so much to lose by having just one little pole down; it can make all the difference between winning and losing. But, having said that, one feels nearly as much pressure with a horse that can jump because then the question is whether you as the rider are going to make a mistake'

Spanish Rider Luis Cervera saw his ambition fulfilled when he managed to persuade his federation to let him compete in both eventing and show jumping at the 1992 Barcelona Olympics. Although Cervera was still better known on the international show jumping circuit – he has been a member of the Spanish Olympic show jumping team without interruption since 1976 – Luis had, in fact, already evented successfully in Spain in 1969 and 1972 becoming national champion on both occasions. Luis found his eventing partner, Mr Chrisalis, in England in the spring of 1991. They qualified for the Olympics by coming fifth at Torino in 1991. In the lead up to Barcelona they won two one day events, stayed clear in Saumur and were placed third at Savernake. At the Olympics they came seventh. Mr Chrisalis went clear but just outside

the time on the cross country and finished the competition with a clear round show jumping.

'Mr Chrisalis has a beautiful temperament. When I was buying a horse, I looked for a safe horse that didn't pull on the cross country which he fulfilled but I also found that he was very scopy and very brave, especially at difficult fences. I love show jumping but the cross country is the real challenge. When eventing, I feel closer to my horse, there is more of a bond because the horse will save your life more than once! You share a sense of survival with your horse. You have to respect your horse much more and save the amount of energy you make the horse spend throughout the entire course. You have to be aware of how much the horse can give you on the day.

'In Barcelona Mr Chrisalis made me feel very secure, as if we were going over a very small course. When I get to the final phase I'm usually more nervous than competing in pure show jumping because I am sitting on a different type of horse. The eventer has run considerably the day before, therefore it is tired and doesn't give you the same sort of response a show jumper would. Sometimes you just have to live with what a tired horse gives you. They have a different way of show jumping and so I let them stand off a little bit, let them travel slightly more to the fences and just hope that they are not going to touch them! In Barcelona, Mr Chrisalis was awful in the paddock, he touched every single fence so I decided not to do too much with him. But then, when we entered the arena, suddenly everything was there; he was helping me, really trying his heart out. It was as if he knew that it mattered. I owe Mr Chrisalis a lot; he had already fulfilled my dreams by getting me to the Olympics and coming seventh was so much more than I had expected'

US rider Dorothy Trapp and Molokai needed a clear round show jumping if they were to improve on their fifth place after the cross country. Going into the final test, the lady from Lexington, Kentucky also knew that if none of her closest rivals jumped a clean round, she could win gold. The pair came up with the required result but so did New Zealand rider Vaughn Jefferis, beating Dorothy who had to settle for the individual silver medal at the 1994 World Equestrian Games in The Hague.

'I was worried about the effect that the cross country day would have on Mo. Not only had we gone very fast but the footing on phase C had been horrendous. I felt a lot of pressure until I started to warm-up. He jumped fabulously, he was off the ground as light as he could be and totally responsive. Mark Phillips is very good at getting me to concentrate on my job and not think about all the pressure. He very quietly got me focused and kept me there during the warm-up. But I will never forget coming down the passageway and reaching the arena when I had a moment of anxiety and break of concentration to say the

least! Mo is probably one of the easiest horses to show jump in that he wants to jump clean but he is not easy for me because riding him is like driving a high performance racing car. He has a lot of gears and is very sensitive. With him you only have to think and he goes. I can get a little anxious and do more than just think, my aids can get a bit too abrupt and this completely grinds the gears. That's when it becomes a challenge for me. I have to be conscious of what's happening underneath me and tune in. During the second half of the show jumping round he saved the day because I had lost it a bit and let the pressure get to me.

'I think he must like me and he has proven that to everybody who has watched us. I know that he trusts me because he had a bad experience the first time he flew. There was a lot of turbulence and he was going crazy. When I finally found my way to him, the moment he saw me he relaxed immediately. It was a lovely feeling to realise that Mo really knows who I am. For me Molokai is a classic Thoroughbred and the reason why people started breeding Thoroughbreds. He's got the heart, the speed, the stamina, the power, the cleverness, the quickness. He is it!'

David Green first rode at Badminton in 1982 when finishing sixth on Mairangi Bay. In 1992 David clocked up his best result to date when coming fourth on Duncan II.

'I just love riding at Badminton. Starting from the load up at home, the driving and then when you first see the house from a distance; it's just a magical feeling. Everyone is on a high and nerves are running at the same time. Words can't describe it. There is just a ambience in the air and really you've got to compete there to appreciate the feeling. It's like when tennis players walk in at Wimbledon. Duncan is just a saint. He has got a heart as big as anything and if you say "Jump", he'll say "How high?". He is an 007 Roger Moore type, he'd go out wearing his tuxedo and never have a hair out of place. He is also one of the unluckiest horses and I'd love to see him do well at Badminton and then I'd call it a day and let him go hunting. Horses do so much for you that there comes a day when you have to say thanks and find another life for them'

Horton Point found his way into the Bevan yard as a six-month-old foal. Before Lynne Bevan took over the ride in 1990, her sister Ros had already shown the horse's potential by being long-listed for the 1988 Seoul Olympics. Lynne and Horton Point went on to win a team gold and an individual silver medal at the Young Riders European Championships in 1990 as well as a team and an individual bronze the following year. In 1992 the pair were placed at Badminton, Gatcombe Park and Burghley, a record no other combination has matched so far. After Horton Point won Badminton in 1994 with Mark Todd, Lynne retired the horse from the sport of eventing and has resumed her first love, show jumping with him.

'Horton Point didn't have much faith in his own ability as a youngster, especially at things like coffins. Jumping him round four-foot-six show jumping courses helped him and once he realised that he had the scope and that we were never going to ask him to do something he couldn't do, his confidence came for the cross country. Horton Point is such a good all-round horse. I have yet to see a horse that can do as good a dressage as he did, be as foot-perfect across country and go out the third day and virtually always jump a clear round. His jumping record is second to none. He is a real gentleman and the perfect horse really. All the show jumpers who see him now just can't believe how well he jumps, especially after having had such a long eventing career. Horton Point feels quite relieved now that he walks off the lorry, has ten minutes' work, goes into the ring, jumps his round and gets back on the lorry. The hours of dressage have finally gone! My dream is to ride him in the Hickstead Derby'

Mark Todd savouring his Badminton win on Horton Point in 1994.

'Winning Badminton on Horton Point was the oddest feeling because I only got to know the horse as a ride at the beginning of that week. The Bevan girls did everything and I just sat on him! He was obviously very well trained and very obliging, a real gentleman. He tried one hundred and ten per cent. He was definitely tired but never stopped trying and kept jumping all the way. He is a real trooper, real workman-like and has a laid-back character but, at the end of the day, he knew he had done something really special. I was happiest for the horse and for the Bevan family because Horton Point means so much to them. They are a fabulous family, very emotional and I went through every imaginable emotion with them, it was just tremendous! After having come so close with Charisma twice and on The Irishman in 1989, I thought that I would never win Badminton again. Horton Point gave me an unexpected opportunity'

WINNING MOMENTS

One of the best moments, which I always try to catch, is the split second when riders show their emotions at the end of a competition. This can be an expression of delight or disappointment – both give the photographer an opportunity to tell a story. However, from a photographic perspective, capturing these feelings is not always easy. It requires a lot of instinct and, as with photographing anything, it calls for anticipation, a quick reaction and that extra bit of luck. Furthermore, compared to other sports, it is quite clear that competitors in equestrian sports don't show any of the range of emotions as freely as other sports personalities, which adds an extra challenge to it. I have always questioned this attitude and can only surmise that those involved with horses are simply a different breed of people. They are more introvert and less demonstrative maybe but primarily humbler because they always credit at least fifty per cent of their achievement to their horse. Another feature is that event riders are much more open than the majority of competitors in the other equestrian disciplines. By talking to the people

Ginny Elliot has won Badminton on three occasions. It was thanks to Master Craftsman that she clinched the famous trophy for a second time in 1989.

'Crafty came really close to winning Badminton the year before, and I felt that, due to my slight incompetence, I had lost the title for him. So winning on him was really special because he is such a majestic horse. I just felt that he deserved to win Badminton as he is one of the best horses I have ridden. He is such a generous horse and I don't think that he has got a bad thought in his head. I felt delighted, not only for myself but obviously for the horse and all the people involved. It's just a culmination of everybody's work all put together. The only sadness is that you are normally so busy that you never really get the chance to enjoy it at the time. I feel very honoured and spoilt to have won Badminton. It's lovely to look back and say, "Well at least I won Badminton and it was tremendous."'

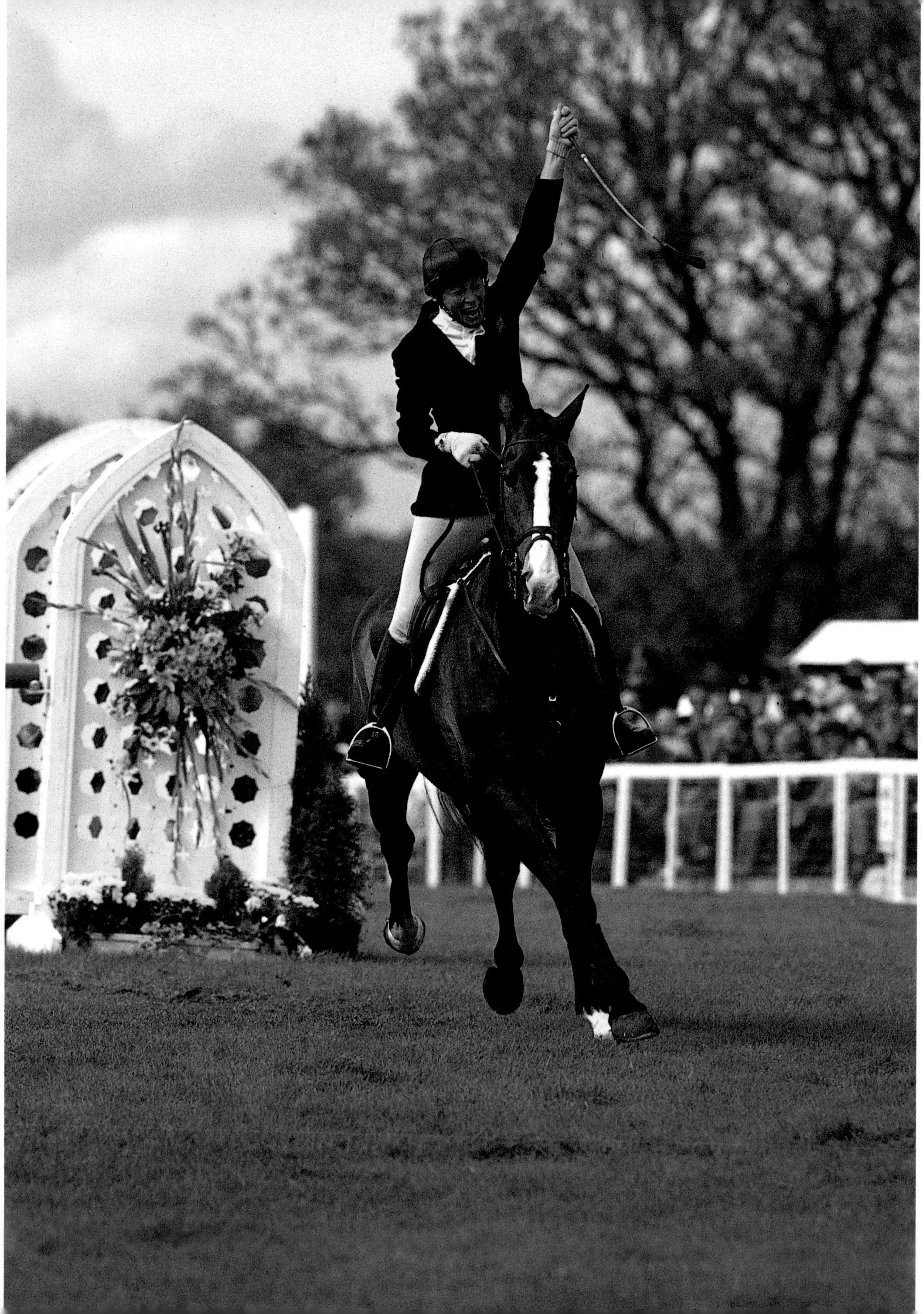

featured in this chapter, I have developed a greater understanding of their emotions, because emotional they are! Yes, they are human but most of the time their feelings are directed towards their horses with whom they spend most of their time. While talking to some of the riders, especially the women, I found out what a close relationship they actually share with their horses. They have a special bond, some of them admitted that they probably know their horses better than their spouses!

In this chapter I have concentrated on those special moments, where riders have demonstrated their delight when winning a major event or championship. Although access to prime positions during prize giving ceremonies can be rather difficult at times, it is wonderful to capture a look of satisfaction on the riders' faces. The elation they feel is proof of the passion competitors have for their sport. Not all riders would show the extent of their joy as soon as they realise that they have won, however, witnessing it makes such a difference and is truly moving! Everything riders have aimed for has

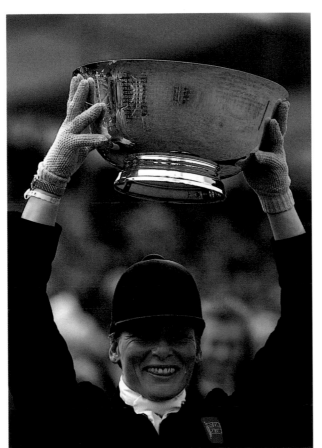

fallen into place and, as they ride through the finishing line of the show jumping course or receive first prize, they can finally let go and celebrate. Often riders are not only showing their delight but also a feeling of relief. All the hard work and tension are over and expectations have been fulfilled.

Many riders say that it usually takes a while before they realise what their win means and it only dawns on them a day or so later. It is certainly not due to lack of support because the crowds who pack the stadiums of Badminton or Burghley are quick to show their genuine appreciation of the winners.

Another satisfying photograph is one where the riders show their gratitude to the horses. Animals do know when they have done their job well and I find catching the horses' expressions very moving. Some event riders will openly share their elation with their horses, especially Juniors or Young Riders.

This book would not be complete without the pictures which capture these precious winning moments.

(Far left) King William gave Mary King 'the best time of my life' when, despite having the penultimate fence down, they crossed the finishing line as the 1992 Badminton champions.

'Winning Badminton was definitely the highlight of my career. It was fantastic, especially as William is so tricky in this phase but he just did enough for us to be able to win. We had also rattled a few fences and I wasn't sure if we had any others down but as we came through the finish I heard the announcer say, "This is the Badminton Champion." I just thought, "Yes, that's it, I've actually won!" It's like the ultimate dream come true. I remember visiting Badminton as a little girl and thinking how could anyone jump these huge fences and here I was actually winning the crème de la crème of eventing'

(Left) Mary King proudly holds aloft the Badminton trophy during the 1992 prize giving ceremony.

'At this moment I was definitely in dreamland. It was like a dream with all the cameras, photographers, interviews, autograph hunters and being crowded by the media. I was in a dream for weeks; you actually wonder whether it's really happening. It only really sank in when I read the newspapers the next day'

Karen Dixon and Get Smart
already had a good collection
of medals, including a team
silver at the 1988 Seoul
Olympics and a team gold and
an individual bronze at the
1991 European Championships
in Punchestown, before
clinching a further team gold
and individual bronze
medal at the 1994 World
Equestrian Games.

'Winning an individual
medal at the Worlds was
really magic and standing on
the rostrum was a fantastic
feeling! I'm quite emotional
about Get Smart because he's
done so much for me. He owes
me nothing and I might have
missed opportunities along the
way, like in Barcelona when I
was told to go round the
houses on the cross country
which frustrated me because I
wasn't able to give the horse a
chance. This time I gave Get
Smart a chance and he came
up trumps! When you have
done everything with a horse
right from the start, winning
an individual medal at a major
championship just puts the
icing on the cake. I know that
Get Smart has done a lot for
the team but to actually also
get recognised and awarded an
individual medal at that level
is fantastic for the horse'

Although US rider Dorothy Trapp felt enormous satisfaction when she won the individual silver medal on her then twelve-year-old Thoroughbred Molokai, the pair had to overcome a dramatic setback on the steeplechase which eventually cost them the gold medal. As they were coming round the first bend Molokai sprung a front shoe, stepped back on it and the nail scraped the sensitive laminae. Because Dorothy was concerned and felt that Molokai wasn't galloping as smoothly as normal, she forgot to check her time on two of the minute markers which meant that the pair collected their first ever time penalties (2.4) on the steeplechase. Luckily a farrier was on hand after phase B to replace the nail and they were able to continue. To make absolutely sure that Molokai was fit and sound, Dorothy dismounted and ran some of the way on the second roads and tracks. After a blistering round cross country and clear round show jumping, Dorothy was eventually able to celebrate their efforts.

'At this moment I was really happy that my parents were present. They have not always been one hundred per cent behind my choice of career but I know that they were very proud of me. It was truly special because I could see them as I was standing on the rostrum. I got Mo from the race track in Lexington as a four year old. He was a promising horse but, after having been crushed coming out of the starting gates, he went down on his knees and from that day he will not gallop in company. From the moment I got him I felt that if there is something that a horse has to have to be a three day event horse, he has got to be it! Mo has always responded positively and been a real trier. No matter how crazy he was at first he was always a joy to ride and I knew that the reason he would get tense was because he wanted to do it right. God taught Mo how to jump, I didn't, all I did was not to ruin him. I did help him temper his overexuberance because he would jump himself into trouble sometimes – I have got a broken collarbone to prove that! But we trust each other and he is definitely my friend which is only natural as we have spent more time together over the past eight years than a married couple would do! Winning the medal made me feel so proud for Mo because I believe that he is one of the best horses in the world. But life doesn't change after a success like that, horses still go lame and I still muck out the stalls!'

The all-girl team of Mary King, Karen Dixon,
Charlotte Bathe and Kristina Gifford were seen as
the underdogs in the eyes of the media before they
arrived at the World Equestrian Games. A great
team spirit, skilful riding and real determination,
together with the necessary bit of luck, helped them
to clinch the 1994 team gold medal in The Hague.
MARY KING: 'Being on the winners podium was a
terrific feeling. As it turned out on the last day, the
team placing depended on how King William show
jumped. Fortunately, he pulled his socks up and
only had two fences down which was enough. My
main concern was not to let the others down after
all the build up and hard preparation.'
KAREN DIXON: 'Winning with the team was fantastic
because of the build-up and we had such a good
team spirit. The unity we had between us was
tremendous. We had been written off by the British
media but that gave us the determination to go for
it, no matter what anybody said. Bad press affects
me in the right way, I get aggressive and want to
prove them all wrong. The win has got to be the
best success I have ever experienced both
emotionally and on a sporting level. I just hope
that we can achieve more wins like that!'
CHARLOTTE BATHE: 'Winning in The Hague was
wonderful, the ultimate really! Riding in a team
means that you have got to go on the course with
the intention of coming back home safe. Mind you, I
nearly didn't make it back home at the second
water and I think I gave everybody back at the ten-
minute box, who were watching it on closed circuit,
heart failure. Coming down the hill to the Hanging
Log fence, I set The Cool Customer up about four
strides out and really kicked him to the fence. He
didn't back off at all but hit the fence which shot
me about six feet up in the air and, as we landed in
the water, he was luckily underneath me!'
KRISTINA GIFFORD: ' There are so many people wanting
to do what we have done and so few who have
achieved it. This makes you realise how very
privileged you are, not only in having the horse at
the time but also being fit yourself at the same
time. Standing on the rostrum and listening to our
national anthem was a wonderful feeling, you
want it to last forever. I could have stood there
all week!'

The newly crowned World Champion Vaughn Jefferis receives a kiss from US silver medallist Dorothy Trapp during the prize giving ceremony of the 1994 World Equestrian Games in The Hague. Before turning his hand to eventing, Vaughn show jumped successfully, qualifying for the 1985 Volvo World Cup Final. However, Vaughn decided not to compete in Berlin because of the long journey from New Zealand and his horse's lack of experience jumping indoors.

VAUGHN JEFFERIS: 'My ultimate goal has always been to ride at the Worlds or the Olympics and I knew that with the right horse the World Championship was well within my reach. As ten-year-old kids, Blyth Tait and I were best friend at school and we used to write letters to one other. When we signed our name we would both put in brackets at the bottom "Future World Champion" and when I won the title my father reminded me of the letters Blyth and I had written! It was a bit of a cliché in fact but also fairly magical because when I achieved my goal I was still a relatively unknown rider as far as the European competitors were concerned.'

DOROTHY TRAPP: 'Molokai had come very close to winning the gold. Even before the competition I thought that if a horse was going to beat Mo it would be Bounce so, in the end, I was pleased that I had picked the right one. It's like when you go to a race meeting and you pick your horse out of the paddock and he wins. I didn't know Vaughn but he seemed to be one of the good guys!'

Rodney Powell partnered The Irishman II when he won Badminton in 1991. The horse had a good track record, coming third with Mark Todd in 1989 and finishing sixth the year before with Rodney.

'The joy of having won something as prestigious as Badminton comes as a delayed reaction. You don't realise that you've won it until about three days later when you get the telephone calls and the newspaper coverage. It was a lovely moment, none the less, and God, would I love to do it again! The Irishman's nickname was Dobbin and, boy, was he a Dobbin; you could trust him with a thirteen-year-old kid. He was pretty laid back; a bit like an ugly version of Mel Gibson combined with the coolness of Robert De Niro'

The combined efforts of Australian riders Matt Ryan, Andrew Hoy and Gillian Rolton were rewarded with the Olympic team gold medal. The fourth team member, David Green, was, however, denied a medal as he didn't complete the three days.

GILLIAN ROLTON: 'When the team won the Olympic gold medal I was overcome with a feeling of amazement. Going to Barcelona we thought that, as a team, we had a good chance for a medal of some sort but to actually win the gold was just fantastic. I felt really proud to be part of such a great team because the guys did a marvellous job. I was lucky to be there. We were such a big surprise to Australia that they gave us a huge reception when we arrived back home!'

MATT RYAN: 'My biggest emotion was a feeling of relief that it's over and that I can finally relax. During the ceremony I was in a little bit of a daze. From watching the video tape I know that I had a conversation with the Princess Royal but I simply can't remember what was said! Winning two Olympic gold medals definitely changed my life. It helped me to raise my profile and to gradually attract more sponsors. But my life had actually already changed after having been round Badminton a few months prior to Barcelona. It's amazing how much respect you get from going round such an event. It was really after that that I started to pick up more rides and Barcelona was just the icing on the cake.'

ANDREW HOY: 'It would have to be the most memorable prize giving of my entire life! I would describe it as an achievement, satisfaction, pride for my country and absolute relief. But it was also the loneliest moment of my career. So many things and so many people have contributed to this success and it wasn't until I was standing on the podium and the national anthem was being played that I was overcome with deep emotions and a feeling of loneliness. I just wanted to run out and grab all the people that had contributed to this. It was similar to when Pat Cash won Wimbledon and he ran off Centre Court to where his entourage was sitting. But I wasn't game to just run off because so many people were back in Australia!'

William Fox-Pitt has had some fantastic moments in Juniors and Young Riders, collecting medals all along the way, but, 'Winning Burghley with Chaka in 1994 has been my greatest achievement so far.'

   'To actually win and not be second or third was fantastic. I was in such shock that I could only manage a smug smile at the time. I was in absolute disbelief that it had happened to me. As I came to the last fence, I thought that he could easily have it down because he can rattle his show jumps and I just urged him to do it for himself, and he did! Chaka is like a little dictator, "Chakaish" as in the Zulu chief. He has also got a bit of Billy Connolly's rough and rugged sense of humour but he doesn't really like anybody. Having said that, he loves my head groom but he and I only do business together!'

The then sixteen-year-old Irish rider Suzanne Donnelly showed her spontanous appreciation after her faithful Irish partner Ballyvaughan Bay helped her to win the 1991 Junior European Title. The pair had to overcome a heart-stopping moment in the water complex at Rotherfield Park but pulled off the necessary clear round show jumping, thereby completing on their dressage score. They were also a major contributing force to the team's bronze medal placing. Since her victory in 1991, Suzanne has, first, taken up science studies and, second, hasn't had the best of luck competing. In 1992 she lost her way show jumping when lying first at the Junior Championship and at the Junior European Championship in Punchestown in 1993 her horse, Speedy Gonzales, went lame when lying first after the cross country. But she still came second with the ever-dependable Ballyvaughan Bay.

'Winning the individual gold medal in England was unbelievable, like a dream come true! Ballyvaughan has an amazing character, he is very kind and has a lovely personality to him. He is easy going, trustworthy and honest. He has every quality you can think of! He tried his heart out across country. His bravery really shone through at the water in Rotherfield Park. He had gone so well all the way which is why I thought of taking the direct route coming out of the water. Jumping into the bounce he must have either fallen into a hole or pecked on landing; either way he went down and I was thrown right up on to his neck, nearly falling off, but he unbelievably picked himself up, threw me back into the saddle and we managed to go on over the bounce! He always seemed to put in that extra effort when it mattered most. In the show jumping phase too we had no fence in hand and I was very focused on wanting to jump my best round because it felt like the opportunity of a lifetime. We had both put everything into it and luckily managed to pull it off! Now I am determined to get a good degree at college so that I can find a job to finance my riding. God gave me a talent and I wouldn't like to waste it!'

The then 21-year-old German Nina Melkonian was the first rider to win both the German Young Riders as well as the European Young Riders Championship in the same year. When competing as an individual at the 1994 Europeans at Blenheim, Nina and her then eight-year-old partner West Star were only in their second season of eventing. Finishing first on their dressage score was more than she had ever dreamed of.

'I had already been terribly thrilled to be asked to travel to the championship so winning the title was unbelievable and I only really registered it once I had come home and my riding club threw a huge surprise party for me. They arranged for a carriage to pick me up in the morning and take me to the town hall where speeches were made and the people celebrated with me.

'I must admit, neither West Star nor I had ever encountered a course as difficult as the one in Blenheim so I was quite relieved not having the responsibility of riding for the team. I always spend a lot of time talking to West Star in the stables before the speed and endurance and I told him that if he felt any of it was too difficult he should just run out and we would ride home immediately. But not once did he give me a feeling of hesitation, on the contrary, we just sailed over everything and it was tremendous fun. It was the nicest, smoothest and most harmonious course I have ever ridden. It was like a dream; I could feel how much West Star had enjoyed himself. He has quite a selfish character, very self-confident and he actually does what he wants with me. We are a real team; I couldn't even start to give him any orders or push him into doing something; we always decide together. As soon as I am too hard with my hand, he simply stops co-operating but when I tune in to him he will do anything for me. Neither of us has the upper hand, most certainly not me! He truly is my best friend and when people talk about the perfect horse and describe all the positive characteristics a horse should have, I always think of West Star'

Badminton 1994 belonged to the Kiwis with the top three places going to New Zealand. MARK TODD: 'It was tremendous for New Zealand! I was glad to have won it! I get along really well with Blyth and Vaughn but, being the oldest one of the three and with all the younger riders coming up trying to knock off your crown, I was pretty pleased to have beaten them.'

BLYTH TAIT: 'With it being in a championship year, it made me nervous because I wondered whether we had had our good luck and left our best performance at Badminton. A good place at Badminton gives you confidence because you know that if you can beat everybody in the spring, play your cards right and prove your performance, there is every chance that you will beat them again in the autumn.'

VAUGHN JEFFERIS: 'New Zealand only has 3.3 million people, of which six were based in England at the time, and then to have three of those take up the first three places at Badminton was pretty special. Personally, I didn't arrive at Badminton with very good memories because of my experience of 1990. I had been eliminated on the second-last fence when my chinstrap had come undone. Nevertheless, I was looking forward to giving it my best shot in 1994 and was extremely happy with my performance'

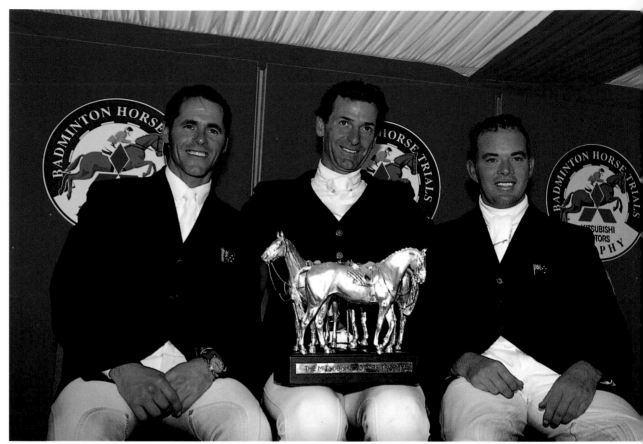

New Zealander Blyth Tait first came to Britain in 1989 to prepare Messiah for the 1990 World Equestrian Games in Stockholm and had every intention of going back home once the games were over. Winning both an individual and team gold medal, however, made it possible for him to find sponsorship and base himself in Britain.

'Winning the world title is what you really dream and hope for. At the time I didn't have a lot of experience on the international scene and I was quite naive in what it was all about. Four years later, with a lot more experience under my belt, I would have probably appreciated and savoured the victory more than I did when I was young and green. I just thought that you went to a competition, did your best and won. Now I know how difficult it is to maintain a team of top horses! I remember being extremely pleased for the team because the main feeling was one of a team effort with everyone sharing in the glory. It was great because the whole team went remarkably well so everybody was in party mood!'

Brittany Ferries

76

LASTING
IMPRESSIONS

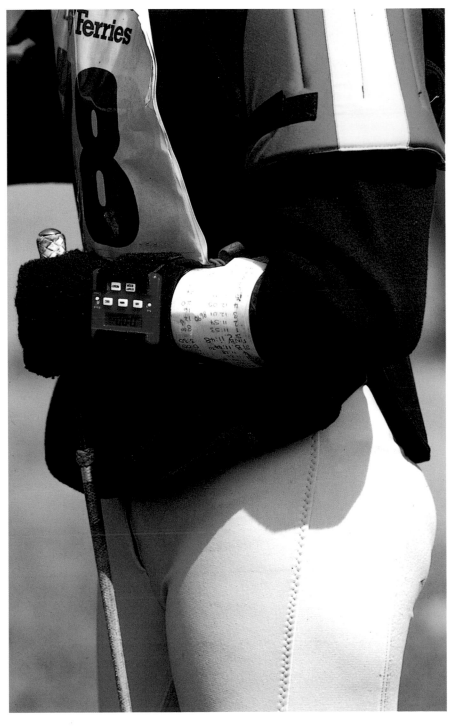

Rotherfield Park, 1991

Bruce Davidson,
Burghley, 1994

Felicity Cribb and Carmody Street, Althorp, 1994

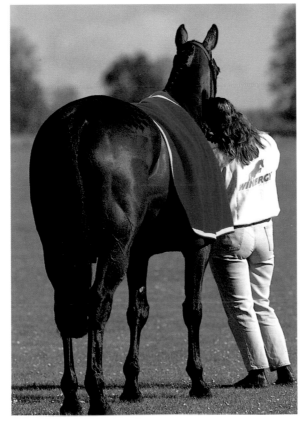

Victoria Latta, Badminton, 1994

Eagle Lion and his groom, Badminton, 1994

Paul Rigby, Windsor, 1995

(Left) Official George
Saunders with his whippets,
Badminton, 1993

(Far left) Heather Holgate
and her black and tan
terriers, Badminton, 1990

(Clockwise, from top left)
Rodney Powell, Burghley,
1987; Ian Stark, 1992
Barcelona Olympics;
Mark Todd, Barcelona
Olympics; Leslie Law,
Althorp, 1994

Mary King, Barcelona Olympics

INDEX

MARINA LOHEIT

JULIAN TREVOR-ROPER

DOROTHY TRAPP

GILL ROLTON

HERBERT BLÖCKER

ROBERT S STEVENSON

PRUE CRIBB

BETTINA OVERESCH-BÖKER

SUE HILL

LUIS CERVERA

HARALD RIEDL

PASCAL LEROY

DANIEL WILSON

ALAN OLIVER

NICKI PARNELL

NINA MELKONIA

ERIK DUVANDER

TANYA CLEVERLY

CAROLYNE RYAN-BELL

DAVID GREEN

PIPPA FUNNELL

DAVID O'CONNOR

LORNA CLARKE

MIKE HUBER

BRUCE DAVIDSON

RALF EHRENBRINK

KRISTINA GIFFORD

IAN STARK

SUZANNE DONNELLY

MATT RYAN

VAUGHN JEFFERIS